Life of Brian

...In Africa

Brian C. O'Donnell

Editor; Frank Sweeney
Cartographer; C. Vrancken

Copyright © 2012. Brian C. O'Donnell
All rights reserved.

Edited by Frank Sweeney
Cartologist: C. Vrancken

ISBN: 147753766X
ISBN-13: 9781477537664

Chapter.	1	Leaving Europe	1
Chapter.	2	Cape going north	9
Chapter.	3	Zambia – Malawi	17
Chapter.	4	Blantyre, Malawi	23
Chapter.	5	St. Patrick's Day, Malawi	27
Chapter.	6	Malawi, Tanzania, Nairobi	31
Chapter.	7	Returning	39
Chapter.	8	Kwacha	43
Chapter.	9	Tom	47
Chapter.	10	Tom/Dan	51
Chapter.	11	Luangwa National Park	59
Chapter.	12	Wattle	63
Chapter.	13	Rocket base set-up	69
Chapter.	14	Kolwesi 1	79
Chapter.	15	Michel after Kolwesi 1	83
Chapter.	16	Foiled hi-jacking attempt	93
Chapter.	17	Leaving for Canada	99
Chapter.	18	Canada to Texas	105
Chapter.	19	Back to basics	109
Chapter.	20	Kolwesi 2	115
Chapter.	21	Evacuation?	119
Chapter.	22	Evacuation U.S. Kolwesi 2	123
Chapter.	23	Diamonds	127
Chapter.	24	Rocket Base to Lubumbashi	131
Chapter.	25	History repeating	135
Chapter.	26	Return, Ilunga, forced stay	139
Chapter.	27	Passport	145
Chapter.	28	Lac Mweru	149
Chapter.	29	Paris, skins, and leaving	155
Chapter.	30	Car mess	159
Chapter.	31	Meeting Fred	165
Chapter.	32	Strange stories	171

Introduction

Monkey Bay

I woke up from a deep sleep in broad daylight, with the sun splitting the rocks. I had slept on my stomach, just like a new baby. I slowly turned over on my back, then realised all was not well. There was an uncomfortable zone below my lower back, and I soon found the problem. There was a bunch of great big fat mosquitoes on the whitewashed wall opposite, happily digesting their breakfast of best Irish blood – mine! I had not tucked in the mosquito net properly when I had to pay a visit during the night, in the pitch dark, without the wisdom of a torch at hand, or electric light, as the generator was switched off at 10 p.m., so now I was paying the price for my inexperience. My arse was a pincushion of bites; - there was no alternative but to live with it – as best I could.

It was February 1975, and I was at the Monkey Bay Hotel, near the southern tip of Lake Malawi. To call the group of thrown-together huts, a hotel, run by an old German, who seemed to be there from the time the Germans left South West Africa after the World War One, was an insult to the industry, but it was the only place there. The Malawi Government shortly after that took over Monkey Bay as a security zone, as their relations with Mozambique, just twelve kilometres away across the lake, were strained, so a second visit at a later date was ruled out. Malawi was the only African country that traded openly with South Africa, making it the political football in the murky world of African politics.

But I digress! I had better begin at the beginning of this travel story, to explain how I got here in the first place!

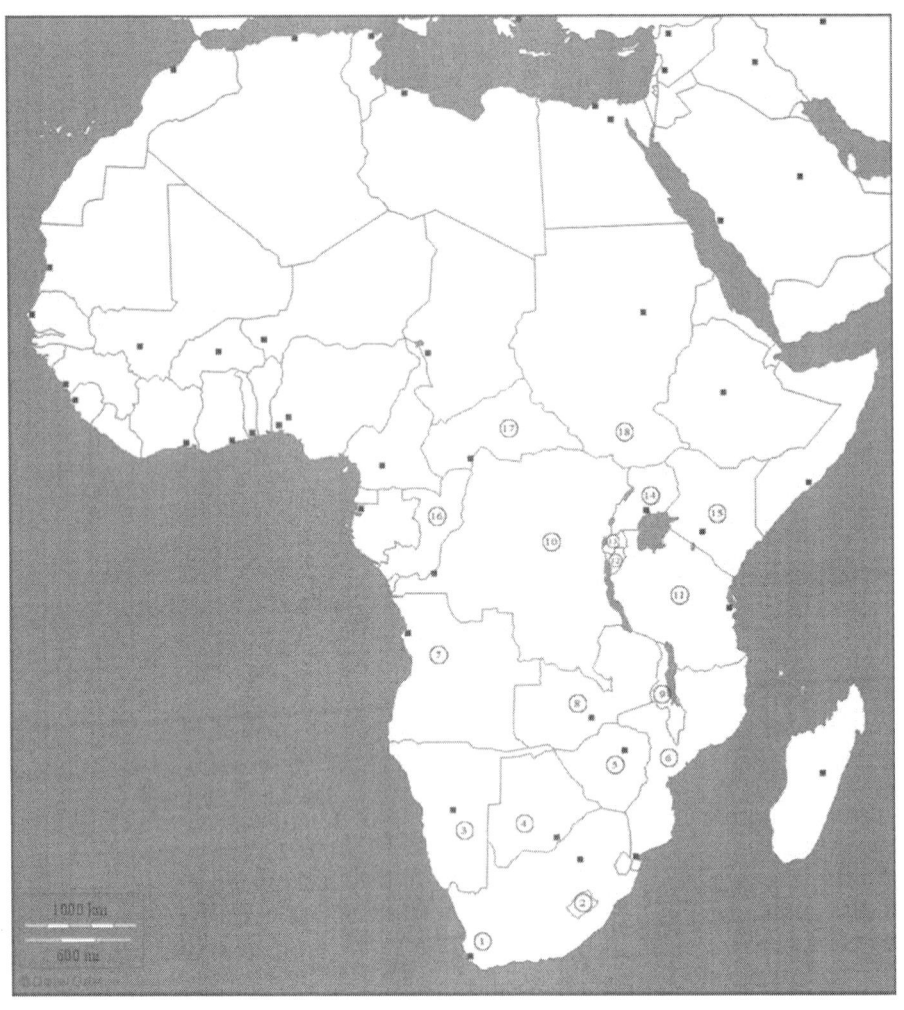

Chapter 1

Leaving Europe

KEY of AFRICA and SOUTH-EAST AFRICA

1. REPUBLIC OF SOUTH AFRICA
Cape Town and Pretoria
2. LESOTHO
Maseru
3. SOUTH WEST AFRICA – now NAMIBIA
Windhoek
4. BOTSWANA
Gaborone
5. RODHESIA – now ZIMBABWE
Salisbury – now Harare
6. MOZAMBIQUE
Dar es Salaam
7. ANGOLA
Luanda

8. ZAMBIA
Lusaka
9. MALAWI
Lilongwe
10. ZAIRE – now DEMOCRATIC REPUBLIC OF THE CONGO
Kinshasa
11. TANZANIA
Dodoma
12. BURUNDI
Bujumbura
13. RWANDA
Kigali
14. UGANDA
Kampala
15. KENYA
Nairobi
16. CONGO
Brazzaville
17. CENTRAL AFRICAN REPUBLIC
Bangui
18. SOUTHERN SUDAN
Juba

    A. ATLANTIC OCEAN
    B. INDIAN OCEAN
    C. MEDITERRANEAN SEA
    D. RED SEA

  a. Lake Albert
  b. Lake Edward
  c. Lake Victoria
  d. Lake Kivu
  e. Lake Tanganyika
  f. Lake Mweru
  g. Lake Malawi
  h. Lake Kariba

It was a Monday morning, dull, grey, in January 1975 with the cloud bank just over two metres from the ground. It was so depressing that one could only be cheerful about it. On my way from my apartment in Eccles to Princes Gardens in central Manchester, my humour just went from really awful to suicidal. By the time I went out for a coffee at 1130 a.m., I had made up my mind – I had to get away from the dreadful climate.

Next decision, where to go to, where one would be in relative luxury, not have to work too hard, have a lot of sunshine, where one could enjoy life a bit? That was easy – it had to be South Africa. A trip to the South African Embassy in London was necessary. I met a very nice man there who gave me a lot of advice and information, and a promise of a ticket on the Blue Train from Johannesburg to Cape Town if I came back the next day, which I duly did. These tickets were like gold dust, with a six month pre-booking, but he was as good as his word. My Blue Train ticket was ready for me, with enough time for a week in Johannesburg on arriving there.

Back in Manchester, I decided to ship my car to Cape Town, as prices there were high, and I could always sell it for ready cash if needed. The only port of embarkation was Southampton, so I arranged for a friend, Alan, to drive it there for a fee of £60, while I was on my way to sunny climes.

South African Airways had a well deserved reputation of looking after their clients. The welcome aboard and the whole procedure of in-flight comfort and well-being of their clients was a pleasure to behold. The food was good, the stewardesses were pretty, and the wine was excellent, so all bode well for the long haul flight.

Due to apartheid restrictions, they could only land at a very limited number of airports to refuel. We landed at Sao Vincente, Cape Verde Islands, off the West African coast. It was just a bunch of sheds, totally under developed, but in recent years, with the discovery of oil, and tourism, it is quickly becoming the place to be for many people. The Boeing 707 was quickly refuelled and airborne again for the last leg to Johannesburg. I mused that here I was again, for the third time in my short life, at thirty five years of age, having a total change of lifestyle. My first was just before my eighteenth birthday, when my father gave me fifteen pounds sterling and wished me good luck. A mini-bus from my home in north west Donegal, Ireland, delivered me at the docks in Belfast, where I got the ferry to Heysham and train to London, a less than pleasant journey, with lurching carriages, and a never-ending 'clackity-clack' of the rails . The complete trip cost me five pounds ten shillings. Sixteen years prior was my first long haul flight, emigrating, to the United States, to New York's Idlewild Airport, now J.F. Kennedy Airport, where my uncle, who had sponsored me, his wife and daughter were waiting to welcome me. I had landed there with £71 in my pocket, after having paid the same for the Pan-Am flight from London, where I had been working at Pinewood Studios as a lighting rigger, setting up the spots and rigging for Liz Taylor who was shooting the film Cleopatra there. Production was later moved to Cine Cite near Rome. It was at Pinewood she met Richard Burton, and she was married to Eddie Fisher at that time. Here I was, starting all over again, a new life, with no idea as to what lay ahead. I was to find out in the next few years!

Arriving in Johannesburg in mid January was a tonic. The Carlton Hotel, in central Johannesburg was lovely, with shopping centres on the lower ground floors, showing a luxury that wasn't in England then. As urged by the 'tourist' man at the embassy in London, I went to the South African Railway restaurant one day for a meal. It was semi-formal, with waiters in starched shirts and jackets floating about, one of whom seated me and gave me the menu. When he came back to take the order, I indicated that I would have a selection of the dishes. Most of what was on the card was new to me, so I hoped that I had not shown up my ignorance too much. That backfired very quickly when he told me, in his heavy Afrikaner accent, that I did not understand, that the card was the menu. I was to get all of it, whether I liked it or not! I liked it a lot, and did it proud, but could only consume two-thirds before giving up. These people here have hearty appetites! The price was embarrassingly cheap. I was back again the next evening for more of the same, and forgot the calories.

I had a few days to do the tourist thing, wandering about, marvelling at the different cultures, foods, ways of doing things, and generally enjoying my new life. While sitting at a first floor bar veranda in one of the main streets, during early evening, the sanitation truck came along. That was a sight to see! It moved along the road at a steady ten kilometres per hour, never pausing, while the team of Africans and Mixed-race ran ahead, preparing the rubbish, a second group picked it up as the truck came abreast, throwing it in the open back, while another few did the swooping up of any bags that were left, running all the time to keep up. It was a pleasure to see such efficiency and teamwork, with the whole street cleared of debris within ten minutes.

I was recommended by a few young Europeans, to go to Santon. It was a rich enclave to the north of town, and the focal point there was a lovely big pub/restaurant, where many Europeans socialised, and the only Africans there were those serving drinks. There I met and was made very welcome by quite a few Whites, who extended their hospitality in their best tradition – very generously.

My day of departure arrived. I was to get the Blue Train at 11 o'clock, and arrived in good time, to be shown on the train to my compartment, which I was sharing with one other European. He turned out to be Swedish of about forty years, more into books and culture than I was, so conversation was polite, but somewhat stinted. The trip was smooth, with the only sound being a faint whisper of the air conditioning. Shortly after leaving the station, the steward came back, gave us the menu, and announcing time for lunch. It was a repeat of the railway restaurant – lots of good hearty food, which we dallied over, time being on our hands. We were travelling through the Karoo, the big flat centre of South Africa, a farming land not unlike the wheat fields of Kansas, was flat as the eye could see, with an occasional Dutch style farmhouse in the distance, inhabited by White farmers of Dutch origin. They had even named the region the Orange Free State, with its capitol Bloemfontein, which lay just west of Lesotho, a landlocked 'independent' state in the mountains. Woe beget any non-Afrikaner who tried to set up house in that area! We spent the afternoon reading. Dinner was an even grander version of lunch and on returning to our compartment, found that the beds had been made up, all ready for turning in, which we did, exhausted.

The next morning, we were awake early, shortly after dawn, and could see the faint outline of mountains ahead. We were coming on to the mountain area, the Great Karoo, which encircled the southern part of Cape Province, with mountains that are not very high, but very similar to the Swiss Alps. A shower, wash, and shave had us both ready for the breakfast carriage. Needless to say, it was excellent, sumptuous. The view from the windows was spectacular. We were now in the Great Karoo, with the train slowed down, winding its leisurely way around the mountains. Some of the railway bends were so curved that one got the impression that the tail of the train was coming to meet the engine. Finally, we came into suburban Cape Town, and got our bags together for the final arrival in the home of the Mother of Parliaments, just twenty four and a half hours after leaving Johannesburg. (South Africa has two parliamentary locations – the original one in Cape Town, the other in Pretoria, where most of the work is done. During their summer months, parliamentary business is done from Cape Town)

As luck would have it, there was a Scottish pipe band on the platform to greet me, playing enthusiastically and with great gusto, great big rousing martial music. After a few minutes, I realised that they were there for another reason – piping off a train load of soldiers to the war in Angola. What a let-down!

It was Tuesday morning, and my car was due any day, so I got a taxi to the docks to enquire just when it was arriving. The harbour office informed me that it would be there on Friday. Well pleased with myself, I was about to leave the docks when I saw a ship of the Ellerman Lines tied up. With a quick instruction to the taxi driver to wait, I raced up the gang-plank, only to be stopped at the top by a seaman, enquiring as to where I was going. I told him that I wanted to see Mr. F., not having any idea if that was his ship or not. I only knew that he was Chief Officer on an Ellerman ship. We had shared a house along with three others in north London up to three years before that. The seaman told me he was in the lounge having his lunch, and showed me the way. There was the bould Mike, in immaculate whites, with a pint in his fist, greeting me with his lopsided grin, and a casual 'bejasus, it's yourself'. After much handshaking, greetings from the other officers, and a promise to meet in Durban, I departed. Mike had a lot of work to do in Cape Town, so I had to bid adieu for the present. Back in the taxi, the driver deposited me in a nice small hotel near the centre of town.

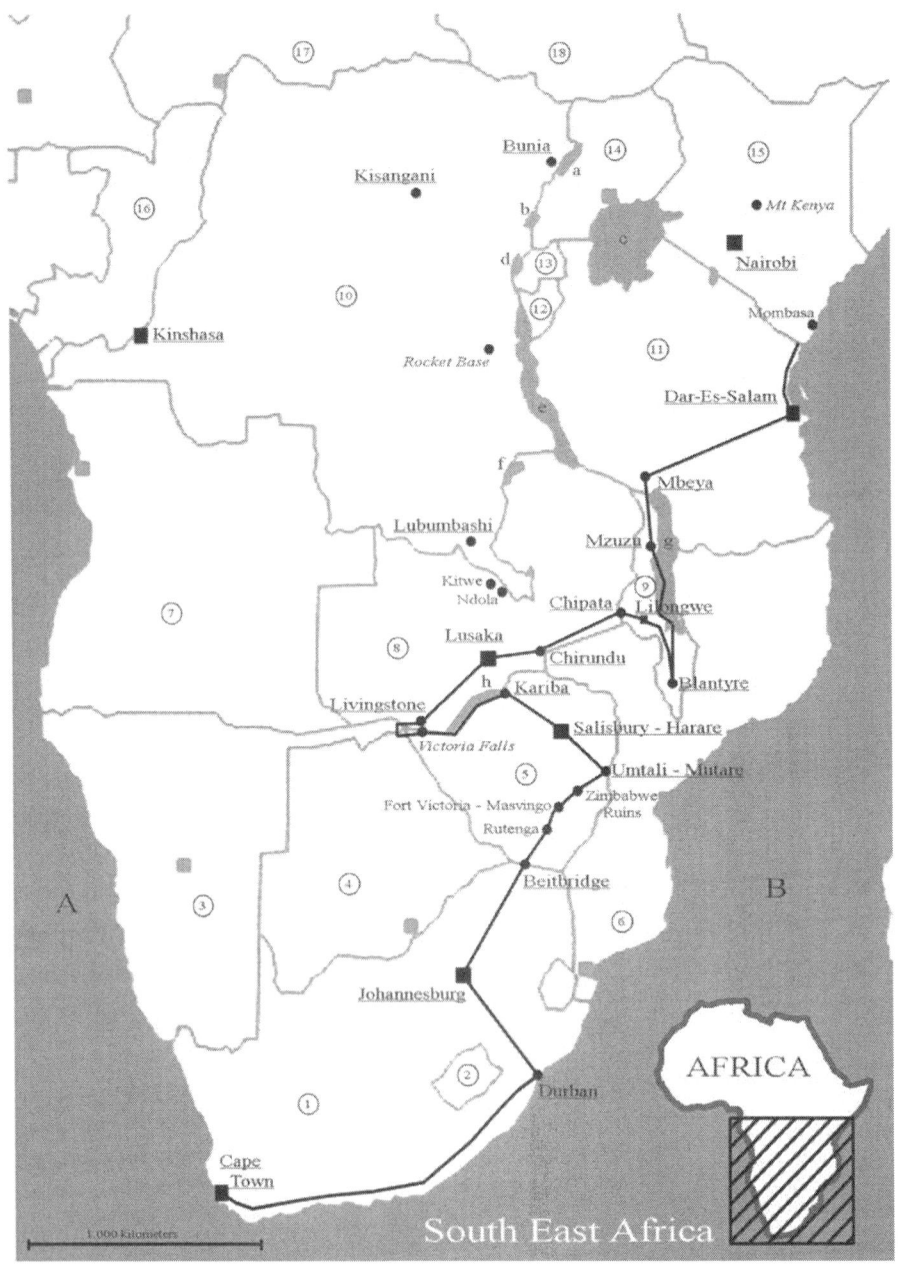

Chapter 2

Cape going north

I spent a few days doing the usual tourist bit in Cape Town, enjoying the lovely sunshine, visiting the largest open-air swimming pool in Africa, where Africans and Coloureds were only recently allowed, swimming off the beach, but only enjoying a quick dip, due to the surprising coldness of the water, a cable car trip to the top of Table Mountain, and best of all, having a good wander to the docks to see the ocean sailing yachts. They were getting ready for the big 'Off' on the Cape to Rio de Janeiro, Brazil, race. There were about twenty large ocean yachts there, tents set up for visitors, hospitality, music, with all sorts of wonderful things for the delight of wide-eyed innocents like me. I nearly had a fight with one particularly uncouth Afrikaner who tried to push his way ahead of me in the line for food, but a good grab and squeeze of his crown jewels made him think again. It was quite wonderful to walk the harbour, wondering at the beauty of the lines of the yachts, and the amount of money it took to have them ready for such an adventure. It was away out of my league, but no harm in enjoying the sight!

CAPE GOING NORTH

My car, a Citroen DS23 Pallas, arrived safely on the Friday, and I picked it up on the following Monday morning, and was on my way to – I did not know where. I had been briefed about the Garden route by the embassy in London, so that was a good starter. I slowly made my way to False Bay, where the shark nets were in place and the water much warmer than at Cape Town, and there, I had a good swim.

Next stop was to Hermanus for the night, where I had a small hotel and my first taste of biltong in a local bar. Biltong is a dried meat, normally ostrich, deer or beef, dried, salted and flavoured, and, as I found out later, excellent as a food substitute over long periods. Next morning, I made my windy way through the Little Karroo to the Cango caves, which were well worth the trip. Acoustics in the caves were amazing, almost perfect, with beautiful stalagmites and stalactites, dripping for thousands of years giving a surreal look to the caverns, and in the greater 'pavilion', concerts are held there occasionally.

The next stop was Outdshoorn, where I had a very enjoyable morning at the ostrich farm, laughing my head off at the attempts of the tourists to ride the ostriches. They had a small saddle placed on their backs with reins, just like horses, but there the similarity ended, as with only two legs, and a long awkward stride, it was almost impossible to stay on for any length of time. I was finally persuaded to try my luck, and now it was the farm hands' turn to have a great belly laugh. Needless to say, my attempts were less than 100 per cent successful. Moving on to Plattenberg Bay, a small village on the coast, with a beautiful beach stretching for kilometres, and a massive multi-storey hotel right on the rocks by the sea, was the next port of call. Since my visit, Plattenberg Bay has been developed enormously, with many hotels, and all the tat that comes with a popular tourist resort. That merited a few days of just lazing about, before moving on to Port Elizabeth.

Going through Zululand, I was intrigued by a group of school children, dressed in their traditional costume of homespun blankets, with whitened faces. I stopped and indicated that I would like to take their photo, and they agreed. Having taken several, they had their hands out for money. I had other ideas, and made a bee-line for the car, with them in hot pursuit. The sight of a bunch of infuriated Africans wielding knobkerries, the traditional stick about a metre long, cut from a knuckle of a tree branch, and deadly in a fight, was a great incentive to flee. Luckily, I was able to get the car in gear and away before they could catch me. Port Elizabeth had no interest for me, being a small industrial town, and as my time was getting short to meet Mike in Durban harbour, I continued right on.

I found Durban to be a big modern town, with tall buildings right on the waterfront, with a fine beach with crashing surf. After checking in to a hotel near the centre, I made my way to the docks, and finally found the Ellerman ship, which had docked the previous day.

Mike was waiting, having off-loaded the cargo in good time, so we hit the town. He was the 'local', having been there several times before, so I was guided by him. We had a great meal, ending the evening in some bar where the walls were covered by signatures of famous people. I declined the invitation to put my own there, near the top of the wall, not from any modesty, but mainly due to the fact that I would be sure to fall off, being too inebriated, and did not want to make a holy show of myself. There was no thought given to drunken driving as we slowly made our way back to the docks, only to find the gates closed, with security not in a humour to admit us. After some discussion, and on playing the Irish card, the guard allowed us in. It was just as well, otherwise Mike would have several kilometres to walk to his ship.

I spent a few days there, swimming, doing a few night clubs, wondering at the high percentage of Indians of various castes who were in business there, until it was time to hit the high road for Johannesburg. The Carlton Hotel in the centre of town was to be my base again. Apartheid was at its peak, with the African and Coloured population being very oppressed. One day, on the street by the hotel, I asked a young local African for directions. The terror in his face had me momentarily wondering what I had done wrong, until I realised his fear was not of me, but of white men, fear that he would be arrested or worse. I was a lot more cautious after that lesson.

It was time to move on, to Pretoria, the seat of government, again doing the tourist bit to the monument of the great Afrikaner trek, before taking the road north for Rhodesia. The road was interesting enough, with little traffic, mostly 4 x 4 farm vehicles with great big grizzly men behind the wheels. It was about five hundred and sixty kilometres to Messina, giving me a taste of distances to come.

The border crossing at Messina/Beitbridge between South Africa and Rhodesia (now name changed to Zimbabwe, and known in the earlier days as Southern Rhodesia) is on the Limpopo River. To the western boundary is Botswana, northern boundaries are Zambia, with Mozambique to the northeast and east. It was a little security conscious as there was a war on, between the 'old' Ian Smith regime, which did not want to give the Africans independence, and the local people, led by Mugabe and Nkomo. Having been to Northern Ireland many times, security was quite low-key in comparison. I decided to take the longer route, in the direction of Zimbabwe Ruins, en route to Salisbury. It had now been a long day on the road, and I pulled over to a lodge at Rutenga, a railroad station. The rail went all the way to Lorenzo Marques, in Mozambique, winding its way at leisurely pace on narrow gauge rails. After a hearty meal, a few beers at the bar, and, despite the heavy presence of security, men in all types of uniform or none at all, heavily armed, all with John Wayne syndrome, I retired and quickly went to the sleep of the dead. Rhodesia employed many mercenaries – people who had fought wars in various parts of the world, and who lived to fight, sometimes to die. They were paid the local army wages, but they were happy doing what they were good at.

Next morning it was a relatively short trip to Zimbabwe Ruins, arriving there well before lunchtime. There was no-one in the area, a complete settlement, now abandoned. There is only speculation as to whom or what tribe built the massive stone walls, some of them more than two metres thick and seven metres high. It seems to have been a secure fortress, with huge circular stone walls, surrounded by larger walls. The complete site was spread over several hectares. It was really quite amazing, and is a complete mystery as to why or when it was built, or where the occupants went. I spent several hours wandering through the 'town', and in that time, never set eyes on a soul. Weird!

Skirting around the southern side of Lake Kyle, the air was very hot, humid and oppressive. The lake was tempting, and as there was nobody in the area, I stopped, stripped off and went for a swim. It was glorious, and I was really enjoying myself, when I felt a bite on my wrist, on the pale skin where my watch normally was. I quickly became aware of the possibility of crocodiles, and beat all Olympic records heading for the shore, even though I am not a good swimmer. Another lesson learned! After that, it was a slow drive to Fort Victoria, where I bedded down for the night in a small local hotel.

Next stop was Salisbury, (now Harare) and the best hotel in town, the Jameson. I was not greatly impressed by the town, but after a few days I had met some Europeans, among them quite a few Irish from Northern Ireland – people who had been there since after the war in Europe, and had settled down to a very good life, mainly in farming.

One larger than life character from my own area in Ireland had a brother in the Irish Government. He was kept at arm's length by the more serious business men, as a person who was up one day, down the next, and maybe sailing too close to the wind for their liking. This man was later to hit the headlines after Rhodesian Independence, when he got a contract from the British Government to supply food to the new National Army being trained by the British Army. He made over six million dollars in six months. Later, President Mugabe wanted some of it, but the businessman refused to return to Zimbabwe until a deal was struck. Despite Mugabe's declarations to the contrary, corruption was creeping in early – a major problem throughout Africa. Meantime, the Donegal man had invested in Irish pubs with his son in Scandinavia, and lived the high life in the Shelbourne Hotel, one of the better hotels in Dublin, for at least six months, until the story broke in the Irish papers. I later met him by accident in the Brussels Sheraton Hotel

– he had not changed. We quickly parted company when he insisted to the bar staff that I was to buy him the best whisky in the bar. I was equally insistent that I was not, and left.

Rhodesia produced excellent tobacco, which was a very important foreign currency earner for the Government, and was auctioned at the end of the season each year. I was urged to go to see it, and it was a real eye-opener. There were thousands of tobacco bales, each about one and a half metres square laid out in several rows all along the length of a huge shed. They had the tops of the hessian bags partly open, with the leaves, some pale vellum, others a dark brown colour, showing for the buyers, who followed the auctioneer as he walked along lines. The auctioneer never stopped his litany, spewing out the prices as he went along, shouting at a terrific rate, without a pause. Every fifteen minutes, another auctioneer took over with the verbal flow continuing without a break. The buyers were shouting their prices, with tally-men noting down just who bought what and at which price. It was all too overpowering for me, but what a spectacle! As the bales were sold, they were quickly picked up on little trolleys and Africans ran with them to the buyers bay, where they had trucks ready for their collection, and slid down the chute to the trucks. Millions of dollars were traded there over the few days of the auctions, and it was an education in efficiency.

I arrived at the holiday resort of Kariba, on the shores of the massive man-made lake, which supplied water to the famous Kariba Dam. The Rhodesian Government transferred many animals to safe ground when the lake was filling up on building the dam. Kariba was a holiday resort with a few hotels. In the bar of my chosen hotel were several tourists from South Africa, who were complaining about not having seen any elephants, when in walked a local European. He offered to show them some, and we all piled into his pick-up. Not far into the bush, we stopped behind a Volkswagen Beetle and another car, watching a herd of thirty-nine elephants cross the dirt track, ambling at their ease, with the massive bull taking up the rear. He stopped right in the centre of the road, looking about him, swishing his tail and trunk, in no hurry. We all waited in wonder, to see what was next. After about five minutes, the driver of the Volkswagen got impatient, and tooted his horn – a high pitched tinny sound. He very soon found out that it was the wrong thing to do – one does not annoy an elephant with intrusive noises. The bull slowly made his way towards the car, all three tons of him, and lifting his massive foot, brought it down on the front of the car, crushing it like matchwood. He then turned and wandered off into the bush, as if to say, 'that will teach you'. It was wonderful to watch, and hilarious. The owner of the car was not so amused, but I'm sure he will refrain from annoying elephants for some time.

There was a ferry going from Kariba to near Victoria Falls, a two day trip. I arranged for the car to be loaded, and embarked, along with about twenty other tourists. The trip was fabulous, with lots of game sightings on the islands on the lake and the shore bank as we sailed by. We heaved-to in the centre of the lake to have a swim, well away from possible crocodiles, and no risk of bilharzia, a disease of African countries, mainly contacted from still water, which attacks the intestines, and is very painful. As there were no car off-loading facilities at the destination, I had to disembark at Deca Drum, where there was nothing more than a slipway for loading and off-loading of boats, and continue on the bush track to the Victoria Falls. A very pretty young English lady, who was on her way with her mother and sister, to study in Australia, accompanied me. We had a very pleasant voyage, and after a four-hour trip, met up with her family at the Victoria Falls Hotel.

Having checked in, with all the pomp of top class service, I went scouting to the nearby falls – the Moshe-y-Tunya – and was awestruck at the power and volume of water cascading over the falls, crashing down over eighty metres below, only to rise again as a mist cloud having hit the basalt rock face opposite, a massive basalt wall, which the water swirled around to the next wall and continued folding around for about four walls before reaching calmer waters, away from the boiling cauldron at the base of the falls. There is a spit of ground jutting out from the Rhodesian side, giving a much better view than from the Zambian side, and it was a perpetual rain forest there due to the mist soaring about a hundred metres in the air, but it was well worth the soaking. The road and rail bridge remained closed, as the Zambians were helping the rebels, and Ian Smith's army did not want to accommodate them.

Travelling to Zambia required a round trip of over four hours each way – going parallel to the south side of the river to the Botswana border, then a short trip north to the river ferry, and crossing over into Zambian territory, before doubling back along the northern bank of the river to the town of Victoria Falls. From about one hundred kilometres I could see the spray from the Falls rising far into the air, giving it it's local name "Moshey-Tunya" – the smoke that roars.

Chapter 3

Zambia – Malawi

It was late afternoon when I arrived at Livingstone, the tourist town on the Zambian side of the Victoria Falls. Zambia got its independence peacefully from the British in 1964, and was then known as Northern Rhodesia. Angola borders almost all of the western side, with the exception of the Caprivi Strip – a very small strip of land in South West Africa, now Namibia, and because of various wars, was one of the most dangerous places on earth. To the south is Zimbabwe and Botswana; north is Zaire (Congo), with Tanzania and Malawi to the east. It is mainly a high plateau, with its main earnings from the vast copper mines near the Congo border. Kenneth Kaunda was president since independence, although born in northern Malawi. Bemba seemed to be the majority language.

The only hotel for Europeans was the Victoria Falls Hotel, where I booked a room for a few days, and met five young Irishmen on the terrace that evening. They were all from Cork, in the very south of Ireland, and had only been in Zambia a week. They were there to set up a safari company for an Irish accountant, who lived permanently in Lusaka, and whose name from Gaelic translated as 'the one-eyed one' or O'Sullivan. Names in

Ireland are very regional, and there were many "one-eyed ones" from the south coast. He was to set up a walking safari company in the Luangwa Valley, where Norman Carr, a world famous old Englishman, had put such safaris on the map. I had a pleasant dinner in their company, with many laughs about their experiences in Zambia.

Next day, at lunch, the smallest and the live wire of the group, calculated the price of the menu, compared with the price of each item if ordered individually. It worked out at one Ngwee cheaper, (one per cent of the Zambian currency, the Kwacha), - about one U.S. cent, to order each dish separately, rather than as the lunch menu. There was great hilarity with the poor waiter on ordering each item, when he tried to explain to us that we were, in effect, ordering the 'menu'. The poor man was all confused, but for his trouble, picked up a nice tip afterwards. That Corkonian's brain was wasted in Zambia. Maybe he came back in the next life as the head of Ryanair, the low cost Irish airline?

I met quite a few nice people in Lusaka, either by the pool at the hotel, or just having a beer at the bar. A few days after my arrival, I met the Livingstone Corkonians again. 'Live wire' was less alive this time – more half dead from exhaustion and lack of sleep. It transpired that he had washed his own smalls himself and hung them out to dry. He then wore them, directly, without ironing. A day or two later he learned of his folly when he started to itch all over. He had the sense to go to the pharmacy for a cure, where they recommended Vaseline to seal the air passage for the grubs that were hatching under his skin, but he was too embarrassed to mention it to his colleagues, and did not put any on his back. The results were soon obvious! His back was a hive of black grubs, merrily eating away his flesh, as they grew big and fat, while itching the life out of him. There was only one thing for it – the slugs had to come out. Such was his discomfort that he did not protest when I told him they either had to be cut out or burned out. That was an interesting afternoon! The 'client' was tightly strapped face down on his bed, with an ironed handkerchief in his mouth to stifle any shouts. His friends were lined up, all smoking like trains, making sure I had a ready supply of well lit cigarettes, while I got on with the job of burning the slugs. After the agony of the first few burns, he became slightly immune, as I popped each slug with the lighted cigarette, totalling more than seventy burn holes all over his back. An hour and a half later, another few lesson learned; – a great introduction to torture, - Putsey flies laid their eggs in the seams of clothing put out to dry, so it was imperative to iron the clothes before wearing them in order to kill the eggs. 'Live wire' had a big glass of whiskey and keeled over, exhausted. I thought I deserved one too, so we all joined in, making short work of the bottle of Jameson, bought only that morning.

I was invited by an Irish couple to stay at their house on a farm, and I accepted their invitation. Mike was an accountant for Lohnro and they lived an enviable life there – a nice house, good weather, safe surroundings, just a perfect place to rear their child. He walked five minutes to work at the office block. It was ideal for a married man with a young family, but not for a wanderlust like me! After a few days, having taken advantage of the car pit at the farm workshop to do a thorough service on my car, I was ready for the next stage – a side step east to Malawi.

The road from Lusaka to the Malawi border was mostly straight – almost one thousand kilometres of boring drive, mainly tarmac. Zambia is mostly a high plateau, with little or no break from the bush stretching to every horizon, with the exception of the Rift Valley where the Luangwa River flows. North and South Luangwa valleys are well known safari areas, where the only way in for tourists is to fly by light aircraft from Lusaka to the various camps there. It is a massive area, low-lying, with the Luangwa River meandering along this lower end of the Rift Valley. It can be sweltering hot just before the rains, when the rivers are at their lowest and all the animals bunch together near the watering holes, making for great sightseeing. To my mind, it still has the best wild life parks in Africa, where walking safaris are the norm. The possible exception being Ngorogoro Crater in Tanzania! Little did I guess at that time that I would be back there later, entering the park, not as a paying guest, but on a more dangerous voyage.

My papers were checked at the Malawi border, formerly Nyasaland, and I was waved through with a friendly smile and wishes for an enjoyable stay. Malawians are a friendly people, kept in poverty by their President, Dr. Hastings Kamuzu Banda, who was a medical doctor in Lancashire, England, and who came back to Malawi at independence in 1964. He always refused to appoint an ambassador to Zambia, as he said he already had one in State House, Lusaka, as President Kaunda of Zambia was born in Malawi. It has little natural resources, with agriculture and tobacco being the mainstay of the society, with Lake Malawi being the real lifeblood of the country.

Next stop was Lilongwe, the administrative capital, built mainly with British aid. Quite a few British worked there on aid programmes, with their own lifestyles transported there, down to a few squash courts. The standard of fitness was quite impressive, playing at lunchtime in 28 Centigrade. Most were well pleased with their posting, as they had standards much higher than that back in Britain, and were treated very well. Food was fresh, lots of fruit at ridiculously low prices – huge avocados cost two tambala (the percentile of the Malawi kwacha) - about one cent U.S. each, tourist price. Vegetables were less nutritious, growing too fast in the heat, unless they chose those from the hill areas. The town itself was without soul, being newly built, purely as an administrative capitol.

Lake Malawi, formerly known as Lake Nyasa by the British who colonised it until independence in 1964, is the southern part of the Rift Valley, and is bordered by Malawi on the western shore for its full length, and on the opposite shore by Mozambique, and Tanzania further north. The lake is about five hundred and seventy kilometres long, but only about forty kilometres wide. Salima Bay Lake Shore Hotel was recommended, so that was my destination. It had a bunch of cabins, well laid out around a central core, with bar/restaurant facing the small beach. By nine o'clock, the sand was too hot to walk on, so it was a race to get into the water before burning the soles of the feet. Many of the ex-pats stayed there, and it was well frequented at week-ends. Some one hundred kilometres further along the lake was Nkhotakota Lodge, a more laid back affair, if that were possible.

A person needs some rest and recreation from time to time, and I figured that I had earned some - which is why I found myself near the Mozambique border on Lake Malawi, at Club Nkhotakota, enjoying the best they had to offer. It wasn't much on the international scene, but there it was pure bliss. A reasonable restaurant, a bar, the lovely lake, great staff, and a mosquito net over my bed! The sun was hot, a dead heat - over 32 Centigrade every day, with the sand on the little beach too hot to walk on without flip flops. Off-shore, about 100 metres out, was a pontoon for sunbathing and swimming. Attached to one side was a ramp, and on the pontoon post by the ramp was a phone. That connected to the bar, and a turn or two of the handle had the genial barman on the phone, taking my order for another Carlsberg. That was delivered when the powerboat started up and the waiter got going on his one ski, floating gracefully to the ramp, delivering my beer and glass on a tray, without ever spilling a drop. This was all done in an immaculate white uniform with a bright red or blue sash diagonally over his shoulder, and taking off back ashore without even getting damp. I had a hard time swimming ashore later, having ordered too many beers, just to see the show.

The hippopotamus pool was 100 metres from the hotel, and the head 'boy' showed me their 'nest'. In the evenings, they gathered in great mud pools at the lake edge, coming from further north with their young, from the feeding grounds of grasslands by the lakeshore.

Next day, having fully recovered after a good night's sleep, being woken by a few bullfrogs making an almighty racket, and a full breakfast, I was ready for anything. It was wonderful to see the hanging nests of all kinds of birds, new to me, just over the water's edge, and thousands of giant multihued butterflies silently flying about, with just too many colours for me to describe with any justice. After some deep thought, I came to the conclusion that some exercise was needed, and what better way than taking a kayak for a spin on the lake?

So, off I go to a small island to explore, about a kilometre out, but as I got near the island, I saw that I could not land as the bush was too thick, and why struggle through God knows what, with an odd snake ready to give me what-for? I gently paddled around the island, and was rewarded by the biggest iguanas I ever saw coming to the water's edge, eying me up, and in their own good time, and retreating back to the safety of the dense growth. Their colours were spectacular, every bright shade possible, vivid as a technicolour dream, and they stretched to a good metre long. The great lake finally beckoned again, and I headed off for distant shores. It was mid afternoon when the storm started up, slowly at first, then the waves getting too big for comfort. At this point, the better part of valour dictated that I turn back. There was one little problem – how to do an about turn in the kayak which had no buoyancy tanks, and was shipping water from the waves coming over the side! There was nothing for it but to try, but with waiting for the lull in the waves and finally trying the about turn, I was left holding the paddle, with the kayak sinking under me. I thought of diving after it, but I gave up that idea when I thought about it – it was one of the deepest lakes in Africa, more than one kilometre deep. Never mind, I still had a stout wooden paddle to cling on to, with water temperature about 28 Centigrade, so it was no big deal to tread water until morning, when I could swim to the shore a few kilometres away. There was no question of swimming there at that time of evening, as the hippos which went up and down from their pool of mud just south of the hotel, did not take kindly to anything in their path. At six twenty p.m. it was dark, darkness having fallen like a blanket, in five minutes flat. About an hour later I heard shouting and finally a light searching for me. A bit of shouting to and fro quickly got the search boat alongside, and a relieved me, on board. I was doubly relieved when my favourite water-skier told me that there were a few, but not too many, crocodiles in the lake. At least they recovered the paddle!

Chapter 4

Blantyre, Malawi February 1975

After a few more days lounging about, getting a little restless at the lifestyle of pure debauchery, I decided to move on, heading south to Blantyre, the ancient capital. The town is at the southern tip of the country, with some industry, exporting to South Africa. Malawi was the only African country which openly traded with the apartheid regime in South Africa, with its claim to fame being the oldest Presbyterian cathedral in Africa. I checked into the Mount Sochi Hotel in the town centre and spent the next day wandering about, finding it a really quiet place, with not a lot happening.

Mount Mulange, the highest mountain in Malawi, near the border with Mozambique, was only a little over an hour's drive, so I set off, map at the ready. Half-way there, coming around a bend on the metalled road, I came to an abrupt halt by a Malawi policeman in full khaki uniform, jacket and shorts beautifully pressed, long socks in a shining pair of regulation boots standing in the middle of the road! How did he get there, in the middle of nowhere? He came to the open window and courteously asked for my credentials. I really had no idea as to what he wanted. His form of questions was new to me, with all sorts of ideas going through my head. He finally

BLANTYRE, MALAWI FEBRUARY 1975

asked for my driving licence and insurance, which I showed him. I am sure he never seen an international licence before, and the insurance certificate from the A.A. was also strange. He went around to the other side of the car, spent a few moments studying the British tax disc, which I had not bothered to renew from the previous December, when it had run out, then came back and handed me my papers. He then stepped back, drew himself up to his full height, and gave a perfect salute with a huge smile. 'Now I have inspected your credentials, you may go, sir'. With a lot of relief, I put the Citroen in gear and took off in a cloud of dust before he realised that everything was not in order. It was a useful lesson for me – brazen it out and all should be o.k. - a lesson I put to the test many times in the coming years, mostly to my benefit. Having arrived at Mount Mulange, I drove the car as far up the mountain track as I could, but then decided it was not worth the walk to the top, and I turned back, keeping a wary eye on the road for my policeman friend. He had vanished just as he had come, out of nowhere.

So it was back to the Mount Soche Hotel in Blantyre for a few gins and tonic. I was becoming quite friendly with this drink. It is made from local sugar cane, and is excellent. Mixing it with tonic gives one that extra sense of righteousness needed for the second or maybe the third drink, knowing that the quinine in the tonic was helping to keep malaria at bay! It was at the bar there that I met an Irish accountant, Cyril, who invited me to dinner at his house one evening. Several days later I drove to his pleasant home in the suburbs, with a well tended garden back and front, and shaded from the road by a high hedge. On my arrival, both he and his wife were very distraught. They had forgotten the dinner, and on offering me a drink, explained the reason why. Three days earlier, the President of Malawi, Dr. Hastings Kamuzu Banda was passing on his way to a dinner of businessmen in the Mount Sochi Hotel. As the entourage was passing Cyril's house, their child of seven years, who had been playing in the front garden, made a loud bang with his toy gun. Immediately, State security was all over the house, and took the boy and his mother to the police station. The boy was released after several hours, but the mother was detained in the high security prison for thirty-six hours. The child was driven back to the house and left there, alone. A neighbour finally contacted the boy's father, Cyril, who was, in fact, waiting for the President at the hotel. Despite being a European of good standing, working for an international company, he was given ten days to leave the country with his family. Such can be the joys of working in a dictatorial state.

Soon after, I headed north, stopping off at the Zomba plateau, a high flat-topped mountain half way to Lilongwe. It is quite a spectacular mountain, rising from the plains to a beautiful forest of hardwoods and grazing land. One can see for many kilometres from there, and sky-diving is popular from the cliffs at the highest peak. The divers must make sure they do not land in the compound of the high security prison, seen far below. Not many prisoners leave there, except feet first.

It never ceased to amaze me how many Malawians were constantly on the roads, going and coming, with the women looking very elegant in their colourful full length dress, carrying a bucket, dish, or huge loads of timber for firewood, going for kilometres. It is a very densely populated country, not much bigger than Ireland.

Monkey Bay was recommended as a pleasant stop-over, so that was my next stop.

Chapter 5

St. Patrick's Day, Malawi – 1975

In my introduction, Monkey Bay is memorable, mainly for my unfortunate circumstances due to my carelessness with the mosquito net, and I spent but two nights there, before moving on. The lakeshore drive going north was very pleasant, but the road deteriorated greatly soon after Nkhotakota Lodge, giving me the first real test of African roads. I finally arrived at Mzuzu, the commercial capital of northern Malawi; sophisticated, with one guest house and a social club, where all the forty-two Europeans in the northern province gathered, mostly at the weekends, to have a beer and converse with their 'neighbours'. They came from farms, aid projects, engineering road and bridge building, to relax, gossip and enjoy a few beers, before collecting their wives or partners and going back to their respective bases for another week of hard work in an alien climate and environment.

  I had a half tank of petrol, but there was no point in proceeding further until I had a full tank as well as full jerry cans, as there were no filling stations for many kilometres. I checked into the guest house. As it was the only one, it was the best in town. O.K. in a poor backpackers idea, but I was grateful for a shelter and bed. Next thing on the list was to fill up with

ST. PATRICK'S DAY, MALAWI – 1975

petrol, so, like a good citizen; I went to the only petrol pump in town. Unfortunately, they were right out, and I was told the next delivery was on its way.

Great, I thought, I can have a night here and get going in the morning. I put my car in the long line of trucks, pick-ups, clapped-out old cars, some wheelbarrows with jerry cans, and God knows what else, to wait my turn. Next morning I was there early, hoping to get going. The reply was the same as yesterday – 'the truck is on its way', coming from Lilongwe, the capital. The penny dropped - the truck would be here when it got here! Some of the roads were difficult, it being the rainy reason, but the short rainy season.

A crowd had gathered around my car staring in at the luxurious Citroen DS23 Pallas, so I did my party piece for them by putting the suspension on low, starting the engine, and then putting it on high, revving the engine, and watching their incredulous expressions and their cries of 'eeeie' and 'aaaie' - as the car went up and down on its hydraulic suspension.

The delay time was estimated as being 'maybe tomorrow', so I took a trip to the lake, a distance of about twelve kilometres. Just south of the little harbour at Nkhata Bay, a small town on the lakeside with a fishing dock, was a small beach. I swam a little, keeping a wary eye out for I don't know what.

As I was leaving, there was a European walking in the direction of the town, and I offered him a lift, he accepted and directed me to the dock, where his little ship was moored. It was one of several small ships that plied their trade all the length of the five hundred and seventy kilometres long lake.

The captain, as turned out, was also an Irishman, from Waterford. We had a nice cool beer or two from his fridge, and in conversation, told me that he had trained horses in Argentina among other things. How he got to be captain of a ship in the centre of Africa was not explained!

I drove back to Mzuzu, and put my car back in the same spot in the line as before, waiting for the tanker. The locals had left my place in line. I was very impressed by their courtesy, something that I found throughout Africa – the poorer they were, the more courteous they were. Next day was a repeat, where I met the ship's captain; we were leaving the beach before 9am to beat the heat, when a longboat came around the point with a group of tourists. The captain told me they were from another small ship which had just arrived. It was the only ship to carry passengers. The first man off the bow to tie up was a big bearded pirate type, who was a vaguely familiar figure.

I wasn't long wondering about that when I heard the broad Northern Ireland accent. He was from Larne, north of Belfast, someone I had last seen on his way to South West Africa to enjoy himself in sand sleighing; - a great sport, but one must not forget to roll off about five metres before the bottom of the giant sand dunes, otherwise the sharp angle at the bottom would be an invitation to hospital, or worse.

As this was 16th March, one day before St. Patrick's Day, Ireland's national day, we three Irish celebrated in traditional manner, even though I strongly suspect either of the two would not be overly keen to do so back in Ireland, possibly being of another religious persuasion. On the 17th proper, every European was at the Mzuzu social club for the big St. Patrick's celebration ... all forty-two of them, including two other Irish, with Larne and myself as guests. A very pleasant evening was spent in the excellent company of the Europeans who had come for the event – it being one of the highlights of the year there. Many of the ladies had brought some of their own cooking, and had laid them out in the centre of a big table, for all to share.

Larne had pitched his tent alongside the guest house, which was full of the bush visitors. He was woken early next morning, when the ants paid him a visit. He had unwisely taken a bottle of beer to the tent on retiring, drank most of it and fell asleep. The beer smell was a magnet for the ants, and luckily had only started on him as he woke up, with bites all over. It could have been worse had they gotten into his eyes or nostrils.

I enjoyed another three days of relaxation, calmly waiting for the tanker, before it finally arrived. It had taken the truck ten days to travel just over four hundred kilometres. I was very kindly ushered to the head of the line to fill up, and despite the short supply, was allowed to fill up completely, including my jerry cans, and head off north to a lot of clapping and cheering. Such was the hospitality of the Malawi people.

Chapter 6

Malawi – Tanzania – Nairobi, March/April '75

It was goodbye to Nkhata Bay and Mzuzu, as the petrol tanker had finally arrived from Lilongwe, the capital, having been delayed by the short rains and impassable roads. I was ceremoniously waved to the top of the line for the petrol, tanked up fully, and waved on my way with much shouting of best wishes. The road north after Rumphi progressively deteriorated, with speed slow to full stop sometimes, to remove big boulders from the track. Several times I was glad of the spade I had bought, allowing me to dig the red marle from the tyres where it had built up to such a coating as to make the traction impossible. This was particularly important as the Citroen was front wheel driven, and on the top of a slope, it was necessary to put the car in first gear, line it up with the track crossing the river, and hope it would not be deflected on the way. I had no wish to slide off the track and end up in the river up to the roof. On occasion, the current was such that I had to wedge open the doors a little, letting the water free-flow across the car as I drove, with a hosepipe from the exhaust to the roof, to prevent water entering the system, and suspension at full height. At least, that stopped it from floating away with the stream. It did not enhance the value of the car having water all over the velour, but that was the price to pay for travelling in Africa during the short rains in a nice car. My stupidity was such and I was on a steep learning curve. I had not checked out anything on travelling in Africa, had no idea of distances; nothing! A trip from London to Geneva maybe helped me somewhat, but Africa is not Europe, as I was quickly learning.

I reached the border post at Chipita, where the road wandered for a short distance into Zambia before touching the Tanzanian border at Mbeya. The Zambian customs' officer was really curious, spending a long time studying my passport, but finally, finding nothing wrong, told me I could enter, but first I had to have immunisation against something or other. He then fetched a syringe with a needle that normally would give a heart attack to a bull, and insisted I must have an arm injection. I was equally insistent that I would not, especially as the hygienic precautions were non-existent. Standoff time! He finally relented after about thirty minutes of arguing, and let me go, saying that I could be in dire danger. In my opinion, I most certainly would have been if I had taken his injection.

A short time after that, while still shuddering at the thought of the massive injection I almost had, I came across a small problem. A Zambian army four- wheel-drive truck was stuck in the middle of the track; up to its axels in mud, with a few soldiers trying to dig it out. They had been there for four days, and had sent a message to their camp for a truck to come to tow them out. I did not fancy a stay of several days, so cleared a little space alongside, with the help of the soldiers, laid a bed of branches, put the suspension at full height, and powered through, much to the amusement of the soldier spectators. Hard to beat French ingenuity!

MALAWI – TANZANIA – NAIROBI, MARCH/APRIL '75

At Mbeya, the border crossing between Zambia and Tanzania was just that – a control point. I had no problems, and was waved through in a few minutes. Tanzania is a vast country, with magnificent plains, the Serengeti bordering Kenya, with Mount Kilimanjaro very near that border, along with Lake Victoria and Uganda to the north, Lake Tanganyika and Burundi to the west, the Indian Ocean to the east and Mozambique to the south. It got its independence from Britain in 1962, formerly known as Tanganyika, and after elections in 1964, Julius Nyerere, a schoolteacher – Baba wa Taifa (the teacher), was elected President. I joined the main Zambia to Dar-es-Salaam road, thinking that such a road must be really good all the way. However, the road was so pot-holed that speed was impossible, and one had to be very careful in overtaking the giant Zambian copper trucks, some with one hundred and forty ton loads. These trucks took five days to do the trip from the Zambian Copperbelt to Dar-es-Salaam, with the single driver going non-stop, staying awake by chewing Betel nut and weaving all over the place to avoid the craters in the road. The Betel nut has 'stay-awake' properties, without which the drive could not be done without several sleep periods. That did not bother the contracting hauliers. The drivers often fell asleep, with the truck veering off the road down the slope into the ditch, where they normally overturned. The drivers were easy to spot later, as their gums were stained red from the nuts, their teeth rotting – a dentists nightmare. It was a common sight to see them alongside the road, with a soldier guarding the long copper one hundred kilo ingots, until they could get a replacement truck. The oncoming traffic was worse, as one had no idea when they would swerve.

I pulled in for petrol at a hamlet and was offered diamonds by a man who appeared from nowhere. I had heard of some cases where Europeans had been suckered into doing a deal, then arrested and everything taken from them by the police who set up the 'honey trap'. That was not for me, so a disappointed plain clothes policeman had no big profit that day!

The small town of Iringa was my stop for the night, in a basic hostel, before heading on the last leg to Dar-es-Salaam. The approach to Dar is a big flat plateau, covered with pineapples, hundreds of hectares of them. I later found that they cost five East African shillings each, but one could buy them in Nairobi, almost one thousand kilometres north, for one shilling each. Such was the socialist state of President Julius Nyerere, who ran the country into the ground, with the support of the USA aid, which distorted everything. Nyerere was, for the Americans, the flavour of the month, and could do no wrong. This was rewarded by a massive injection of aid money, mostly squandered on such projects as the pineapple fiasco.

(The Zambia – Dar rail link was being built at this time by the Chinese, who made a deal with the Zambians for mining and trading concessions. The rail line started in central Zambia at Kapiri Mposhi, about one hundred and eighty kilometres from the Copperbelt, and ended ten kilometres from the port of Dar – something I will never understand. The Chinese did not employ any local people, had their own camps, never ventured among the locals, and even had their own prostitutes imported from China. They were greatly detested by the locals. That was the beginning of the great Chinese colonisation of Africa, which has since been expanded all over the continent. The railway is at the time of writing, virtually non-existent, with very few trains running, and being kept alive through misplaced national pride.)

I found Dar-es-Salaam uninteresting, with low-rise buildings, and the whole town built around the port. There were about twenty rusty ships lining the docks, with more on the skyline waiting for a berth. I did not delay long enough to check it out, but continued on my trip north to Kunduchi Beach, which I had heard, was worth a visit. I booked into a local hotel, right on the beach, and decided that it merited a few days rest. The sand on the beach was pure white, and I thought of going for a moonlight dip, but the hotel owner advised me on venturing out on the beach after dark – too many muggings. As usual in Africa, the sun set very quickly, shortly after six o'clock, and a leisurely dinner was one way to pass a pleasant evening, followed by a nightcap.

Work started early, just after daybreak, and the place was bustling, with the owner and a helper getting ready for a fishing trip. They were to catch tropical fish, and he showed me his holding tanks, getting ready for the next air shipment to Germany. He put a few fish in plastic bags with water, and sealed the bags after blowing oxygen into them, enough for their long trip to a tropical fish shop in cold Europe. He invited me to go part of the way with him and his helper, in their pirogue, a dugout made from the trunk of a tree, and dropped me off on an atoll while they fished. It was just heavenly – all alone with a few palm trees, lovely soft sandy beach, plenty of shade under the trees! I dozed, swam, and sun bathed for some hours until I was collected again.

This pattern continued for several days until he had enough for his consignment. I then had a look around the locality, and was particularly interested the local Makonde tribesmen who were famous for carving wood figures. The Makonde habitat area extends from Mombasa in Kenya, along the coast of Tanzania to the north of Mozambique. Their carvings were really sophisticated and intricate, and on enquiring from one who was carving under a tree by the wayside, as to who or where he got his ideas from for the unusual shapes, he told me that they came to him in dreams, some the devil, some good. The Makonde have a very special ability to create such shapes, which I have not seen anywhere else. They keep mainly to themselves and the 'old' ways. After the normal discussion and haggling on price, I came away well pleased with a few pieces.

One afternoon, a four-wheel drive truck arrived at the hotel, full of trans-Africa tourists. This was the same group that I had met briefly in Blantyre. They were tired of sitting in the back of a truck coming all the way from Johannesburg, and some were well fed up with their travelling companions. They pitched tents, and settled down for a meal after a good swim, and we all enjoyed a pleasant evening's conversation.

It was time to move on. By now, I imagined that I would stop my travels in Nairobi, sell the car, and fly back to London, to do something? The road meandered along the coast to Bagamoyo, with Zanzibar in the distance, through Pagnani and on to Tanga, where I stayed the night. Opposite was Pemba Island, and the coastline was just like something out of a glossy magazine. The road from Tanga got worse as it progressed towards Lunga Lunga, the Kenyan border post on the way to Mombasa. Weaving between the potholes was a pain. I was running low on water, as I had neglected to top up, thinking that I would be in Mombasa quite soon. Silly me!

Some ten kilometres later, there was an ominous clatter from the left front wheel. Disaster! The steering bushings had given up, and try as I might, overalls on, with the car jacked up, there was no way I could get the job done. I needed professional help. Help was on its way however, in the form of the ex-army truck hovering into sight. They stopped, all in sympathy, and gave me some much needed water. The only solution was to be towed, which the driver kindly offered to do, and soon we were on our way to the Kenyan border. The driver explained to me that he could not take me beyond the border, as his job would be in jeopardy. I was glad of the offer, and accepted without hesitation. Rope was secured, and we took off, and I mean, took off, at about fifty kilometres per hour, with me trying to signal the truck to slow down, to no avail. The inevitable happened. I pulling over as best I could, while being forced forward in tow, trying to avoid a bus coming my way, but this still left me too close! Unfortunately, the bus driver must have been on drugs, as he swerved to my side to avoid a large hole. He did not judge it well enough. I was holding the wheel, hoping he would miss my car, when the door beside me took off in a great spinning motion, flying in the air and landing in a field twenty metres away. I was left holding the steering wheel, not believing my luck in not being dead, and it flashed through my mind of a Charlie Chaplin situation in one of his silent movies. We all stopped, looked at the damage, which was, miraculously, very little. The door had been taken clean off its hinges, with not a scratch on any paintwork along the body. We collected the door and heaved it into the back seat. There was no point in taking names, or any action against the bus company, as it would be a waste of time. There was no damage to the bus, with its big steel bar across the front to deter people like me from hitting them. After some words of sympathy and a handshake, we all continued our journeys. I was still in amazement of my good luck in not being killed.

The unscheduled stops had the truck driver a little late, so he took off again at a cracking pace. He did not appreciate my difficulties in trying to steer while being towed at about sixty kilometres per hour on a narrow potholed road, but finally, after a hair-raising twenty minutes, I got the truck to stop. The driver explained that he had a schedule, was already late, but sorry, could not slow down. It was that or nothing! I choose nothing, rationalising that it was better to be alive doing nothing than dead being towed behind a crazy driver. It was the parting of the ways. A few hours later, sitting in the shade, wondering what next, a bus came along, going all the way back to Dar-es-Salaam. Saved once more – the Gods were beaming on me that day, and so I arrived back in Dar late in the evening, with nothing to show for my trip but a broken-down car. The next day I found a garage which was AA recommended, that promised to collect it and send it to Nairobi. I imagined that it would be able to be repaired in Nairobi easier than in Dar. With that done, I took an East Africa Airways flight to Nairobi.

The airport at Nairobi was then a bustling place, full of tourists from Europe coming to enjoy the many game parks, and the sun, safaris, and beaches. Kenya got independence peacefully, after the earlier Mau-Mau war, in December 1963, with Jomo Kenyatta, of the Kikuyu tribe, from the slopes of Mount Kenya, as the first President. It is a huge country, a tourist paradise, producing excellent tea and coffee to the north of the capital, Nairobi, on the slopes of the perpetually snow covered peaks of Mount Kenya, near the equator line. Swahili is widely spoken, with the main tribes being Kikuyu, Maasai on the savannas and Luo towards the Ugandan border, while the coastal region is mainly populated by people of Arabic influence, speaking Swahili, who originated from the Omani peninsula. Swahili is spoken all along the seaboard to South Africa, with a simplified version, Ki-Swahili, being used mainly by Mozambique miners in the gold mines of South Africa.

I chose the Intercontinental Hotel as my base, and I luxuriated by the pool there for a few days, doing the sightseeing thing, visiting the Norfolk Hotel, where all the backpackers gathered, while putting their notices on the tree which grew in the lobby, in the hope that they could contact friends, sell equipment before heading back to Europe, or find a companion to share travel with. It was a lively spot, with young people of all nationalities chilling out, sipping their beers to make them last as long as possible. It was a different scene in the interior bar, which did not allow 'riff-raff', where the white Kenyans, and the black Kenyans who wished to be white, hung out. Shades of times past, when the Whites were looked up to and admired, now going to seed, with some old timers still holding on to the illusion of the Empire and all that entailed for them in bygone days.

Some days later, the Overlanders truck pulled into town, the end of a long trip for most. Some hardy characters were going all the way to Europe, across the Sahara desert, but most had enough roughing, coming all the way from Johannesburg.

One young well spoken lady of the group asked me if she could have a shower in my room to get some of the grime of the travels out of her system. I lent her my key, and afterwards we had a beer, sharing reminiscences. She was Scottish, not a Londoner, as I had thought from her cut glass accent. Her father still lived on the island of Mull, off the west coast, and she visited often. I mentioned a name of a neighbour of mine in Ireland who was dry ditching there, who had a big article in one of the Sunday papers some time previously. She immediately replied that she knew him, he worked for her father. Small world!

Chapter 7

Returning

I really enjoyed myself in Nairobi, sunning, nightclubbing, and visiting the United Services Club, a little way out of the centre of town. The Services Club was a throwback to the old colonial days. I just could not believe it the first time I visited. There was a long bar, armchair seats where old men had their brandies and cigars, and snoozed after lunch, polo grounds and tennis courts, and all the paraphernalia surrounding a 1920 style gentleman's club, down to the old fellows sleeping off their lunch in the library, which was a men-only lounge .The mostly ancient clientele were holding on to the last bastion of the old days –'must keep up our standards, old boy' – being their excuse. In reality, they were living a dream, had no more ties with Europe, mainly England, as most had come out after the Second World War They had a good life acting the big Bwana and generally lived well. It was time for me to head back to reality – whatever that was or might be, but not for them.

On a later trip, I met a fellow Ulsterman, Jim, a cousin of a past Prime Minister of Northern Ireland. Jim was a really nice man, who invited me to stay with him on his farm. I spent several weeks there, in the Ngong Hills,

RETURNING

where he bred horses. One of his biggest headaches was the loss of horses to lions; another was a great fondness for 'uisce beatha' – the water of life.

My car had arrived as the garage in Dar-es-Salaam had promised. I had thought I might never see it again. It looked forlorn, stashed away in the corner of the yard of a big garage, showing the worst for wear, with the velour seats and the carpets in a mess, owing to the water flowing through the car at river crossings, and the driver's side front door still where I had left it, on the back seat. . I instructed them to try to sell it, but as it was almost a one-off there, it would need a particular type of client.

I booked my flight with British Airways to London, getting a good deal on the last seat available. My funds were running low, so I went to the Standard Bank to change my last travellers' cheque. Standing in line of the cash desk, with people moving in and out of big doors open either end, to let air flow, I waited patiently. I failed to notice a young boy slowly approaching, and when he was within reach, he grabbed the cheque from my hand, and did a runner through the other door, followed closely by myself. I followed him through several streets, in and out of shops, then into a multi-storey office block. He obviously knew where he was going, and gave me the slip by going into several offices, and disappeared. Two days later, I saw him on one of the main streets, he saw me, and the chase recommenced, but he had a head start, so I soon gave up. £100 to him! He probably needed it more than I did.

Finally, the flight to London took off, a BAC 111, with engines in the rear, right beside my ear – noisy vibrating things – not at all pleasant. On landing at Cairo for refuelling, taxiing to the bay, I was looking out the window, thinking the plane was going very close to an Egypt Air parked 707. Two technicians were working at the top of the steps at the front entrance. They were not there for long. With commendable agility, they flung themselves into the open door as the tip of the BAC111 hit the windscreen of the Egypt Air plane, deflected off that, and swiped the heavy steps from the plane, losing a piece of about twenty-five centimetres from the tip of the wing. A shudder went through our plane. I called to the stewardess that there had been an accident, where upon she told me to be quiet. Wrong answer! I told her, not so quietly, that we had lost part of the wing. By now we had arrived at the refuelling bay, and the captain came to have a look. After about ten minutes we were told that we would have to disembark for a while, and they very generously offered a voucher for a sandwich or a coffee or tea. I was underwhelmed by such generous expenditure, and made my thoughts clear on leaving the plane. The six hours we had to wait was spent quite pleasantly talking to the stall holders in the airport, even though it was clear I was not buying anything. They were very interested in where I came from and asked many questions. I did not need a voucher or pay for the tea they kept offering me. Meantime, the flight crew were quietly going around asking the female passengers if they had any red lipstick. Having assumed we were waiting for another plane to arrive from England, I now realised we were going back on the same old tub, with the wing tip covered in plastic, painted red, which is just what happened!

Finally, we were called to board, and while the plane was getting ready for departure, I waited at the door, cooling off. When the captain came aboard, I accused him of the accident being his fault. His face went a bright red, saying the other plane was 'parked too close'. When I pointed out that the other plane was parked, he, taxiing, was at fault, and mentioned that the best thing he could now do for the passengers was to offer free drinks all the way back to London. He redeemed himself a little by doing just that as soon as we were airborne. Now I know where the slogan 'the world's favourite airline' comes from. Well done, British Airways!

First on the list was a few days 'rest and recuperation', just to get over the previous six weeks in Nairobi, and get back to the swing of life in Europe again. A few pleasant days passed, spending a lot with a cousin and his family. He was a chef in a hotel, and as a sideline ran, a Chinese restaurant in Soho, in the heart of 'clubland' London. Some Irish will get up to the craziest things! Then it was back to Manchester to give notice to my landlord, and clear out my flat in Eccles, and within three weeks of arriving back in Europe, I was on a Zambian Air flight to Lusaka.

Africa had got into my blood, and I could not bear to think of staying in Europe. Nothing for it, but to go back to Africa – to Lusaka, Zambia, where I thought there were opportunities to replenish finances. Arriving there, I checked into the Pamodzi Hotel, and went along the Cairo Rd. to explore the town. The central divide on Cairo Rd. was a tourist trap, with many ivory carvings, malachite, and wood carvings for sale to the innocent tourist. (One could only export goods valued at a maximum thirty Zambian kwacha from the country, so many got caught by customs, and had to hand over their carvings at the airport.) I very quickly met a few Europeans around the pool and at the nearby Intercontinental Hotel.

It was obvious that there was a big black market in the local currency – the kwacha. People with hard currency bought the local money at a huge discount on the black market, making life for them a lot easier, and cheaper. There were very few Europeans who did not avail of the opportunity to change hard currency for their local needs, leaving their salaries mainly in Europe. It did not do a lot for the country, but bribery and corruption was rife.

I wasn't there long when I met a South African who was married to an Irish woman from Dublin. He was manager in a store in town, and lived on the company farm some kilometres south of Lusaka, where he invited me to stay with them. It was a lovely place, a big house on a high hill, with views to as far away as Kafue, many kilometres south. Clive and I got on well, and as he was as anxious to enrich himself as I was, we hatched a plan for export of some kwacha. I knew there was a market in Antwerp for them. The only challenge was to find enough and to smuggle them out.

Chapter 8

Kwacha

Clive knew quite a few Europeans who were in Zambia for years, and who were keen to get some 'real' money in a bank in Europe, rather than hold the non-convertible local currency. A deal was done on the exchange rate, and they were to give him a large sum of Zambian kwacha in the largest possible denominations. By this time, the Zambian security was wise to smugglers, and was trying to stop the trade. If one was caught, it meant many years in jail, with bad food, chain gangs, and all the pleasures that one could expect there. Anyone changing large sums of money, or trying to buy large sums in big denominations, were suspect. Clive's contacts assured him that all would be O.K. on the day. It wasn't!

He was running around like a demented mosquito trying to get all the cash transferred to big notes, instead of the ten kwacha notes he was given – a risky job at the best of times, but we were under time pressure, with the flight to Brussels already confirmed. In the end, we had enough small notes to fill a suitcase. A bright idea, or maybe a crazy one, was decided on. We bought a big Tam-Tam, - the big African drum used as a communication tool in the countryside, - a good one-and-a half metres high, took the skin off from the top, and stuffed the hollow inside with the notes. It was a tight fit, but we made it, with ten centimetre space at the top, to give it some semblance of resonance, in case anyone was curious enough. The skin was replaced as new. I headed for the airport with the drum, luggage, and a plastic bag with some malachite and a few ivory pieces which I bought on Cairo Rd. – just to distract attention. During pre-boarding, customs asked the usual 'anything to declare', and I promptly told them of the drum (slung over my shoulder and impossible to miss) and the plastic bag. When he asked me how much I had paid, and I told him it was a total of fifty kwacha, the man was delighted! I had committed an infraction, and I could see promotion stripes in his eyes, as I was allowed to take out only thirty kwacha worth of good. I was suitably contrite, and offered to give back some of the malachite or ivory, but he was having none of it. In a last desperate effort to get things moving before they took me to an inside room for full search, I offered the drum. The senior Custom officer then came over to see what the delay was, and on hearing the problem, just shooed me through. Just as well, because at that point, the cord on the drum was really digging into my shoulder. A big sigh of relief! My distraction had worked.

However, that was short lived. Going across the tarmac to the plane, the head of State Security, a prick from Belfast, was amusing himself by banging the face of a European against the side of the plane, by the open hold door, demanding that his 'guest' point out his suitcase, in order to recover it. Luckily for me 'Belfast' was too occupied to see me mount the rear steps of the Boeing 707 beside him and on to the plane. I felt sorry about the poor European with the blood splattered face, but glad it was not me. 'Belfast' would have put me in prison and thrown away the key. I even refused the stewardess's offer to put the Tam-Tam at the rear in a space for bulky parcels (that was pre restricted baggage days). A further little hitch occurred when the captain announced a delay in take-off, due to the unorthodox use of State power by 'Belfast'. Thirty anxious minutes later he had announced that either we leave in the next ten minutes, or we would have to get a flight the next day, as he was near to his working time limit. It seems 'Belfast' did not get his suitcase, but the European missed the flight, and we were airborne. All went well, with my colleague-in-crime and I having few drinks before settling down for the long flight to Frankfurt, then Brussels.

I had previously gone through the procedure used at many airports that we were likely to use, and had checked out Frankfurt as not being a problem. Unfortunately, my information was a little out of date!

Frankfurt – new airport, new procedures! We had to disembark, and when re-fuelled, go through customs again before going on the last leg to Brussels. The nice lady at customs admired the Tam-Tam, remarking on its weight, whereupon I gave her a quick run-down on the qualities of this 'hard' African wood, Mukwa. She even remarked on the nice tone, little realising that there was only ten centimetres of empty space inside.

Brussels airport was no problem, and we sailed through. At the hotel downtown, we could not get the skin off the drum, so Clive went out and bought a hunting knife and proceeded to do a good hacking job on the cow skin. A big holdall was necessary to take the loot to Antwerp, to the heart of the diamond area, where the money changer, Leo, had a nice currency exchange business at the front office. When the front office man was satisfied as to the business of the visitor, dealers were allowed to proceed to the back office, where the real business was conducted. There he did the necessary calculations, and paid us our share in U.S. dollars. He had clients waiting for this type of deal, who would pay him for the smuggled money, and take it back to Zambia. Private enterprise is a wonderful thing! We got our money, Leo got his percentage, the Zambians/Nigerians/Malians and Senegalese got their money, and all were happy, with the cycle starting all over again, in reverse.

(Unfortunately for Leo, he hit the headlines some years later, in 1988 when the Finance Police raided his place, and put him in jail. I had seen both his big safes open in his back office. They were stacked with many gold and silver kilo bars, hundreds of thousands of dollars, and monies of various currencies, waiting for the right rate to exchange them for his clients. The mainly African clients trusted him implicitly. I do not know what happened when the raid was made, but am sure none of those clients came forward to claim any of it.)

At a later visit, 'Belfast' 'invited' me to his office, asking me what I was doing in Zambia, and finally showing me mug shots. I recognised one or two, but pretended not to. One in particular was a Greek who had a restaurant in the diamond area of Antwerp, whom I later visited and mentioned that he might be a guest of the State if he returned to Zambia.

Chapter 9

Tom '75

Having made a successful trip on the first such venture, I was ready for a repeat operation, so very soon I was back in Zambia to search out more money. With all the foreign mine workers in the Copperbelt, I reasoned that that was the place to be. Many of the towns there, along the Zaire and Angolan borders were built by the mining companies to extract copper, and in doing so, built townships to cater for the ex-pat employees, along with social clubs, sports grounds, etc. The Europeans were mainly paid in Europe, with a certain amount paid in local currency. Many were willing to fund other European visitors expenses with local currency, in return for an agreed rate paid to their bank accounts abroad. This enabled them to deplete their local holdings, while giving a good rate of exchange to the visitor.

I was waiting at Lusaka airport, Zambia, for a flight to Kitwe, a mining town in the north, in the Copperbelt! For once, all was going smoothly, I checked in without problems and the plane was on time for take-off. We all, a full compliment, trooped out in single file across the apron to the plane, and then it struck! One of the front tyres was flat. 'Sorry, but we must change the tyre'. No one objected, as we thought it better to wait a little than have a crash on take-off or landing. The tyre change took several hours, not a Formula 1 best time, but eventually we all finally trooped back on again, fastened seat belts, ready for take-off. The Captain, after welcoming us aboard, apologising for the delay, told us of a change of destination, to Ndola, as there were no landing lights in Kitwe, and it would be night by the time we arrived. Anyone who cared to get off and wait until the next day's flight could do so. That only invited a rush by about ten Zambians, getting out of their seats, gathering all their bags (this was before the days of mini-luggage), getting their luggage from the hold, and presto, before one could say 'Chillabombwe', we were airborne. Landing in the dark was no problem in Ndola, with its well lighted runway.

Zambian Airways had organised to take us by taxi to Kitwe. Not the usual nice air-conditioned taxi one could get at Frankfurt, just any old car that that had enough petrol, and looked like it could make the journey. The distance was about one hundred kilometres, known, as I later found out, as the most dangerous road in the world. It soon became obvious why, as I sat in the front seat, squashed between the driver and a big Afrikaner. The road is dead straight, no pun intended, through the forest – the blackest forest I ever saw. It runs just south of the Congo border. And very close to the spot where Dag Hammarskjold, the U.N. Secretary General, was killed when coming in to land at Lubumbashi during the U.N. intervention there in Katanga in 1961. (There is a monument erected to his memory at the spot. During a later trip, I went to visit the monument, some little distance from the main road, along a forest track. I was relieved to see that the Zambian authorities seemed to be keeping it in reasonable condition. I said a prayer for their eternal rest, one of whom, Mr. Hammarskjold's personal bodyguard, was a friend of a friend. The U.N. were in Katanga in 1961, and their chief there was an Irishman, Conor Cruise O'Brien. Later, when I went there, giving my name as Brian, the Africans immediately replied "ah, O'Brien". I quickly put distance between myself and O'Brien, but was amazed that they could remember that name fifteen years later. Obviously, he had made an impression! It was at that time that the opposition leader, Patrice Lumumba, was killed with the connivance of the Belgians and American C.I.A.)

Along the main road, at various intervals, were huge trucks on the road, some in the middle, but all without a light to warn one of the dangers. The Kamikaze Zambian drivers just went hell-for-leather, as fast as their motors would go, and were often too late to stop before going under the tail of the loaded, unlit trucks, many with one hundred and forty tons of copper. The result was carnage, with most of the occupants being decapitated! The trucks were hardly ever serviced, and the transported copper to Dar-es-Salaam harbour in Tanzania, was a trip of five days non-stop. The drivers kept awake by chewing Betel nut, a kind of drug that kept them awake and pumping, until they collapsed.

The drivers then took two or three days rest, before heading back again. It was a regular sight in Zambia and Tanzania to see these giant trucks, all manufactured in Brazil, tipped over, where the driver had fallen asleep, or gone too close to the edge, spilling tons of copper bars all over the place. It was then the job of the army to guard the precious cargo until another truck could be commandeered.

Amazingly, we all arrived at the Edinburgh Hotel without incident. Then the fun started – a near riot for rooms, until the hotel manager finally lined us all up, and called out the names of those who had booked rooms. I had booked a room by telex, so relaxed until my name was called out, and a tall well-dressed man went to claim my room key. I produced my telex, and as it turned out, he was one of a dozen without a booking, who chanced his arm, but he had an illustrious surname, the same as mine. What can one do in such a predicament, except offer a fellow white man the spare bed which was in the room? We conversed for hours, he telling me he was from Billings, Montana, one of five brothers. It ended fairly well, he doing his thing, me doing mine, which was to contact some Europeans about 'relocating' their local currency, and we agreed to meet in Zurich at a later date.

Chapter 10

Tom/Dan

Before departing the hotel in Kitwe, Zambia, Tom, my new friend from Montana, doing who knows what, and myself, arranged to meet in Zurich. He was always a snappy dresser, always anxious to give the impression of being a man of some wealth, and he chose his hotels accordingly. He was staying in the Nova Park, Zurich – one of the biggest hotels in Switzerland, a short tram ride from the town centre. When I had finished my courier work to Antwerp from the Zambian Copperbelt, I got a flight to Zurich to see Tom. He presented me with ideas to make money, along with some of his 'ongoing' projects. This sounded music to my ears, and I agreed to team up with him.

We moved into an apartment in the hotel, which would suit us fine, where we could discuss at our leisure, without too many nosey observers, and allowing us to come and go without interference. It was a pleasure for me, with a good swimming pool in the basement, alongside a big Turkish hammam. There were five bars in the hotel. The horseshoe bar on the ground floor quickly became my favourite, where the excellent English barman would discreetly let me know which of the many pretty young ladies were free. Many of them were married, but their husbands were too busy making money for the Swiss banks to look after their wives. A few minutes later, a drink was being offered by him from me, invariably resulting in the chosen lady joining me for the evening. What a great way to meet the locals!

One friend of Tom's, from London, came to visit at Tom's request. Mike was a likable fellow, short of stature, but with massive shoulders, and a bushy beard, with a rapidly receding hairline. He looked every bit a tough man, but came across very well. Apparently they had met during some deal in London, and Mike was in awe of Tom. We arranged for Mike to go to Zambia to buy ivory from the Government stock at Chilanga, or anywhere he could, sending him off with a bunch of money.

(I later learned from Mike a little of his past life. He had done two years prison in England for drug smuggling, where he had been caught taking in drugs from the Caribbean in a yacht he owned. The yacht was still moored in Barbados, and he was interested in trying to smuggle drugs again. I was having none of it, mainly because that is one thing I refused to touch, having seen some of the devastation caused to people who had succumbed to drugs, but also the likelihood was good that the authorities had placed a bug in the yacht, making it highly dangerous for anyone trying to smuggle anything.)

Chilanga was the official warehouse for all Zambian ivory, either taken from poachers or from periodic culls in the game parks. There were up to four hundred tons of ivory stocked there at any time, all recorded and referenced. Zambian ivory is some of the best in the world, and it was an impressive sight. This was during the period that the animal rights people were kicking up a fuss, and the Zambians were waiting to see what the outcome of international wildlife rules would be.

Zambia later burned about two hundred and fifty tons of this ivory, to appease the World Wildlife people. It would have been better to sell it on the European market, ensuring some control, and use the funds for their own needs. Poaching continued unabated. In Kenya, when President Jumo Kenyatta died, his wife, Mama Ngina, was effective ruler. She had teams going out in the game parks, shooting the elephants from helicopters, almost completely decimating the herds of elephants in the country, earning her a fortune from the tusks, tons of which she had shipped directly to Hong Kong. That was the main entry point for raw ivory, the gateway to China, where it was intricately carved and much prized by the Chinese for centuries.

When things moved in our line of work, they moved fast, and one had to move quickly to avoid missing out on a deal, or potential deal. Other times were just boring, something I normally overcome by sightseeing, or sipping coffee or beer on a terrace in the Haupbanhof while in Zurich, observing the ladies passing by doing their shopping in the chic stores nearby, while they, like me, whiled the day away.

During one of these lulls, Tom asked me if it would be possible for him to get an Irish passport. His parents were both from Ireland. His mother was from mayo, had immigrated with her parents at fourteen years of age to Canada, and a year later had moved over the border to the Klondike town of Billings, Montana, where she met and married Toms father. He gave me a copy of a newspaper cutting from the local paper in Billings on her death, which I sent to a friend in Dublin who worked in the passport office. I got a reply ten days later, telling me that his mother was not born in the named town land, but was born twelve miles away, two weeks later. In the reply was a letter from the Department of Foreign Affairs for Tom to bring to the Irish Embassy in Geneva for his Irish passport. He was a happy man several days later when he returned with a spanking new Irish passport.

One day, I decided to move a little further afield, and took the train to Lucerne, a beautiful town on the lakeshore south of Zurich, with two covered bridges across the lake. From there I took the funicular train, one of the steepest in Europe, to the top of Mount Pilatus, where there was a restaurant with outside seating, giving magnificent views over the adjacent Alpine range. I was disgusted to see someone had scribbled their names on the fencing which had only just been installed, and not yet even painted, and was surprised to see that the names were of two Irish girls, with their addresses and phone numbers. I copied details of both in my diary, and on my way back decided that I would have some fun with the two miscreants.

I sent postcards from every country I visited, with the exception of Switzerland, to the older of the girls, who was twenty-three years old then, making a play of trying to catch Jim Figgerty, who, mysteriously, managed to avoid capture at the last moment every time. (Jim Figgerty was a fictitious figure in great television publicity by the makers of Fig Rolls, a biscuit much loved in Ireland. Everyone was talking of the wonderful adventures of Jim, and I am surprised that the idea was never resurrected for another advertising campaign.) The postcards were sent for about two years, until I was based in Houston, Texas. A few years ago, on my retirement, I came across the old diary among a lot of old papers, and wondered if the person was still at that address, so I dialed the number in the diary. The area code had changed, but with the help of the phone company, I was soon speaking to a lady who gave me the numbers of her brother. When I explained that I had been abroad for many years, and wondered about his sister, he gave me her numbers in Dublin, where she now lived, and her married surname was the same as my own.

I phoned her, asking if she had ever been to Switzerland, and when she, surprised, answered in the affirmative, was even more surprised when I asked if she had ever been to Mount Pilatus. She agreed that she had, wondering where this was leading to.

The bombshell was not long in coming! I told her that she had written her name on the fence post there, and it was a fixed penalty, which she had never paid. Her protests that this was the first she had heard of it fell on deaf ears, with my telling her that the Swiss Government wanted their money. Her protests that it was a matter for her lawyer had no effect, with my telling her that as the interest had accumulated to over ten thousand Euros, the Swiss Government then gave it to bounty hunters, - I was that man, and wanted the money! The next few minutes were interesting, with her nearly having a heart attack on the phone, until I decided to take her out of her agony, got her calmed down a bit, and then asked her if she ever received postcards from someone who was on the trail of Jim Figgerty? She immediately replied that she had, and still had them, quoting me verbatim from one, explaining that she was ready to go on the web to see if she could ever find out who was the nutcase who had sent those cards. She also called me more than a few choice words for giving her such a fright about the fine, but we hung up agreeing to meet! I have not yet had the courage to face her – maybe some day? At least that will have cured her of writing on fences in Switzerland.

Things moved slowly from Zambia, with only one small consignment coming to the warehouse in Antwerp, with Mike phoning from time to time, assuring us that all was well, and the big deal was on its way. I made a trip back to Zambia to speed things up a little, to get more ivory out. The flight was via Nairobi and Dar-es-Salaam, to Lusaka with East African Airways. At Dar, a stunning reddish blonde lady took the seat in front of me, dressed to the nines, as for a film set, with full safari gear, even including the pith helmet. On take-off, she asked for a white wine. I started quietly smirking to myself at her naivety – no way was she going to get white wine on a flight that was flying by the skin of its pants! Much to my surprise, she got one. I quickly asked for the same, only to be told, 'sorry, all sold out'. Served me right! My affront was soothed on landing at Lusaka, where the stunner seemed lost, waiting in the line for exchange control. Being ever helpful, I quietly asked her if it was her first time (what a line) and we got talking. Apparently, whoever was to meet her had not turned up, and she was completely lost. It was Independence Day in Zambia, so the local office was closed, and they did not bother to check if anyone was arriving. Of course, being gallant, I offered her a lift to the hotel in the car driven by Mike who was waiting for me. She worked for the Ford Foundation, and was later going to Mogadishu, then to Addis Ababa from there. I pointed out that there were no flights from Mogadishu to Addis, and she came up with the bright idea of hiring a Hertz! It was a journey of over one thousand kilometres across mountains, no filling stations, war, etc. Finally she decided to fly back to Nairobi, then to Addis. Americans have no concept of difficulties one can encounter in Africa, nor any idea of distances. We became good friends from there, and I visited her in New York City several times, where she lived on the Upper East Side. We corresponded regularly, with her writing to my sister's address in Dublin, where I collected a bunch of three years replies to my letters, during a long absence.

All went well with the ivory, having acquired five hundred kilograms from the Government stores, for export. All the paperwork was in order, with one small hitch! There was no export permit, even though they insisted on and had been paid in hard currency, and had given a letter that all was correct for export. Just another little challenge to be overcome! Matabisch – big brown envelopes, - were the answer, and very soon the consignment was on its way to Natural Warehouse, Antwerp. I was also on my way there to conclude the deal, but this time took a UTA flight to Paris, and had my money paid out in two days.

All was going smoothly until a phone call from Mike upset the applecart. Tom was on the phone a long time, and when he explained to me that Mike had bought a furniture factory with most of the cash, I grabbed the phone. How the lines did not melt all the way to Lusaka, still remains a mystery. It was five o'clock in the evening Zurich time. I was on the Zambian Air flight two hours later, on route to Lusaka. I checked into the Pamodzi hotel before eight a.m. and began searching for Mike.

By a stroke of luck I met an African acquaintance in central town, and he was able to tell me the location of the furniture factory. I bulldozed through there to the office, where the surprise on Mike's face was as good as a tonic. It was a Thursday, and two air tickets were on his desk for a trip to Livingstone for the weekend. They were quickly confiscated, and a refund later received from Zambian Airways. There was a little explaining to do! It turned out that Mike got funky by being there without a work permit, and to legalise himself, bought a furniture factory. Putting it that way, I suppose it made sense; if one was completely mad, stupid, or both. Needless to say, we parted company, not as the normal bumph usually says, 'on amicable terms'. What to do with a useless factory? I sold as much of the lathes and other machinery as I could, and walked away from the deal. About a year later, I met Mike's live-in girlfriend in London. She was very attractive, but she surprised me by telling me that he was gay. One lives and learns.

Back in Switzerland, Tom and I often had meetings by the bar in the apartment living room, mostly with friends of Tom's, nearly all looking for finance for some way-out scheme or other, which was going to make us a fortune overnight. My s...t detector was usually working overtime at these meetings, with my input normally being 'why us'? This annoyed Tom at the beginning, until he realized that the question worked, with most of the flakes not able to give a rational answer, they packed up, and left.

One such scheme Tom was very interested to hatch was one where fake diamonds would be manufactured over the border in Austria, in a laboratory, under very high heat and pressure, giving a finished product which very much resembled the real McCoy. Then these 'diamonds', were to be sold to U.S. servicemen at their bases in Europe, giving a false certificate with the signature of one authentic international verifier who had agreed to sign the certificates for a substantial sum. By the time the scam would be discovered, when the sucker brought it to a jeweller back in the States, we would be long gone. I wanted no part of a deal where Uncle Sam, or the International Crime & Drugs Administration, had an alert out for me.

(Years later, when I had settled down in Belgium, I spent a week with a relative and his family, as his guest in their house in Rome, where he was the British head of their International Crime & Drugs Team there. I really got a kick out of staying in the compound which the British took over from the Gestapo just at the end of the war, about five hectares of gardens, with a few houses for the senior embassy staff, and the ambassador's residence. There was a walled swimming pool there which was built for Hitler, but he never had the chance to use it.)

One day, when Tom asked me if I minded if his brother Dan came to stay for a few days, I agreed immediately. I wish I hadn't. It was obvious from day one that he was a lush. Tumblers full of Polish vodka at 11o'clock in the morning were not my style of doing business – especially our business, where one had to be alert and on the ball at all times. He had been fired from his job as vice-president of something or other in California for being a drunk, and now was freeloading off his brother.

I brought up the subject with Tom once or twice, pointing out that we could never use a person like that who would be totally unreliable. Against my better judgment, I agreed to have him stay while Tom went to Rome for a few days on an unspecified trip. He gave me the name and address, with phone number to contact him if necessary, something I thought unusual at the time. The hotel turned out to be one of the most exclusive in Rome.

The morning after Tom left, I suggested to Dan that I would do some shopping, and we could eat in the apartment. I was gone forty-five minutes and on my return, had an immediate feeling the apartment was empty.

There was no sign of Dan, and a quick check confirmed his luggage missing. I tried to rationalize this, as Dan was not a traveller, being on his first trip outside of the U.S., and did not speak any language other than American. Caution suggested that I check the strong box. My fears were confirmed. The box was empty, with Dan gone to enjoy the spoils. Things then started to click …I had been set up! Tom was in Rome with an alibi and I was responsible for the cash … all the working capital.

As Dan did not speak any language other than English, I figured that he would have gone back to his home grounds, the U.S. A quick check with the Swissair desk in the hotel lobby confirmed that there were two flights to the U.S. that afternoon, and that he had booked a flight to Chicago. I immediately took a taxi to the airport, and asked the Swissair desk there to get the police, but not to announce over the Tannoy public address system that I was looking for their passenger who had just checked through. Of course, the P.A. began screaming for Mr. Dan to come to the Swissair desk as someone was looking for him.

To put it mildly, I was furious, but it was too late. Just then the police came along, and it took a few minutes to convince them that I was serious about the missing money. We went through security to the plane. All the passengers were on board, ready for takeoff. I was urged to be quick in my search of the plane to try to pick Dan out, but I missed him in my hurry. The police had his luggage taken off and the plane departed. There was no sign of any money in the luggage. Obviously with that much cash – U.S. 120,000 – he kept it close to his chest, in his briefcase.

Tom arrives back at my request, making a good show of being all confused as to what happened, while quietly thanking his lucky stars his brother had gotten away with the gains. He later used the theft as a reason not to repay an Australian who had given him money for speculation. The Australian later wrote to me in London, but I got no reply on trying to contact him in Sydney.

Tom professed to be completely baffled by the whole deal, but not put out as much as I thought he should be, which only confirmed my suspicions. That was the beginning of the end of our partnership.

The police were curious as to where Dan had gone, Tom having declared him missing. They interviewed me twice, thinking, as they said, that I had murdered him. I pointed out that it was I who had nearly snared the thief, and eventually they did not pursue it further.

Two years later on going through Zurich airport, I was 'flashed' going out the security doors. The security had me on their books still, so I kept a very quiet weekend doing the tourist thing.

Tom's ex-wife, who lived near Pretoria, South Africa, confirmed to me while on a social visit to her parent's house about a year later that Dan had died in California with Tom at his bedside. Enough said!

A few years later, in 1984, while I was working out of Houston, Texas, Tom phoned me at my office, suggesting we have a coffee. I think I made it clear that that was not a good idea! What gall!

Chapter 11

Luangwa National Park, '76

Like a drug, I was attracted again to Zambia. I reasoned the place I had some experience of by now was my best bet. I was back in Lusaka, had bought an old Land Rover, and had got a team of four together to go to the ultimate location – Luangwa National Park, near the Malawi border. There are two national parks there – South and North Luangwa, and are among the best wildlife parks in Africa. Their inaccessibility and being part of the Great Rift Valley made them ideal for wildlife, warm and with plenty of water. To get into the game camps visitors were usually flown in by small plane, and the camps were closed during the rainy season.

Having left Petauke, in eastern Zambia, not far from the border with Malawi after ten days waiting for the river waters to subside, we got near the 'back door' of South Luangwa National Park. Luck was on our side. Nearby, there was a 'folly' built by a crazy Englishman years previously. As he was long gone to meet the here-after, it was now being run as a Zambian hotel. We were not the only guests. There were two young Zambian girls waiting for a bus to Ndola, in the Copperbelt, a journey of two days, having just finished their schooling not far from the hotel. They were good fun for a few days, but I decided to use the waiting time to check out a Government motor auction in Lilongwe, the new town built some years previously in central Malawi. I was gone for several days, and on my return, the Copperbelt bus had been and gone in the interval. The floods had subsided sufficiently to allow us to continue our long- delayed journey. One of the men was to go in the Land Rover to the park gate and start chatting up the guards. This was helped by two crates of beer. Meantime, myself and two others were to circumvent the gate, walking a bush trail, and make our rendezvous with poachers about three kilometres inside. The meeting was successful, with a fine haul of very big tusks, two of which were the best I ever saw – 22 kilograms and 23.5 kilograms. Elephant tusks are rarely the same size, owing to their foraging with the left tusk, wearing it down somewhat. There was a lot of sweat and swearing in carrying them to the meeting point around the park gate, taking care to make a good detour of over two kilometres. Another trip with the full complement of men brought a full load in the long wheel-base Land Rover, and was covered with hessian bags to try to hide the contents. I slept on the roof of the Land Rover, while the others had make-shift hammocks, with all well hidden in the bush from view of any casual by-passers.

The next day, it was the start of the long haul, over six hundred kilometres to Lusaka, but first we had to pass the Luangwa River Bridge, where a permanent Zambian army unit checked all traffic doing the crossing. The solution was fairly simple – trucks from Malawi were constantly on the run to Lusaka with grain, and a dollop of matabisch (an Arabic word for backhander or 'brown envelope') to a truck driver we chatted up at a stop about ten kilometres before the bridge ensured our booty was well hidden in the middle of the grain. One of our two cars went ahead of the truck, while I came along five minutes later, in the empty Land Rover. All got across the bridge without incident. The goods were collected about twenty kilometres further on, the Malawi driver was paid for the transporting of the ivory, and we were on our way, with a clear run all the way to the capital.

So we thought! We had forgotten the Tsetse-fly control point about half way. The sole guard came out of his rondavelle, a traditional African hut, enquiring after our load. It was so obvious, there was no point in telling white lies, and I told him it was ivory tusks. He asked me to wait a minute. I had the choice of driving through the barrier, or waiting. As he was alone, there was no reason to make more problems – until he came out with an ancient Lee-Enfield .303 rifle, stating that I was under arrest. At this point, the two Zambians in the front of the jeep (the back was chock-a-block with over a ton of best Zambian), flashed their cards – Special Police – and declared that I was already under arrest, and they were taking me into Lusaka. I thought 'now I am in a right pickle'. The Tsetse fly guard sprang to attention, highly impressed, and declared grandly, with his best salute, that we were free to go. It took me all of ten minutes along the road to realise the two Specials were not in the least interested in arresting me – just getting their share of the ivory in the back. I laughed all the way to Lusaka.

The next problem was to pack the goods for air-freight to Europe, and what better place than the furniture factory that we had invested in – thanks to Mike! We were able to stock the load there in a secure room, and have several sturdy boxes made, the ivory well packed, all ready for shipping. The only other small detail was shipping clearance. This was secured by the help of a compliant customs' officer, who, for a sizeable consideration, was willing to pass the freight as malfunctioning medical machinery, - a fairly common occurrence in this corrupt society. All went like a dream, the shipment arrived at Antwerp, Willy did very good business, and I got paid. I was not so happy this time with my dealings with him, as I had an impression of being taken advantage of somewhat.

Chapter 12

Wattle '76

On a passing visit to London, I picked up a magazine which had a story on Lohnro, and was intrigued by the report on Rhodesia Wattle Ltd., one of their companies. Having been there, I was curious, and read more. Amongst mining, farming and engineering as well as other things, Lohnro had a tanning enterprise in the Eastern Highlands, near Umtali, bordering on Mozambique. They grew one hundred thousand tons of Wattle trees each year, which matured in twelve years, cut them down, stripped the bark for tanning, and then, unbelievably, burned the wood in situ in the mountains. I contacted the London office, to be told that the Salisbury office was the place to contact, which I duly did.

    They wanted a letter outlining my idea, which was simply not to waste the wood. They quickly invited me to Rhodesia, and I paid them a visit on my next trip, via South Africa. I met the big boss of Lohnro in Umtali, gave them a quick run-through of what I proposed. I was to take all the stripped wood from Lohnro for free, haul it at my cost to Umtali, make charcoal of it, and ship it to Middle Eastern countries, where they barbeque meat a lot, and where wood was in very short supply. The end result would be good for everyone. Lohnro would be seen as going the 'green' route; I would get the wood for very little cost, and make a profit by shipping it out twenty thousand tons of charcoal briquettes to a market crying out for it. A win-win situation for all!

Lohnro gave me a parcel of land by the rail line for the burning station, a turnkey set-up which was to come from USA. Research had shown that there was a company in Raleigh, N. Carolina, which manufactured such turnkey machinery. Wood was fed into the jaws at one end, burned at a low heat for twenty-four hours, coming out as good quality charcoal briquettes, then paper-bagged and sealed, ready for transporting.

All seemed good, ready to roll. I asked to go to the mountains to see the wood for myself, being a bit incredulous that they burned a good wood just to gain bark. I was taken there by three hefty gents in a protected Land Rover. The protection was necessary, due to the many land mines and bombs laid for the military by the rebels, in their attempts to win the war. The border with Mozambique was only a few kilometres away, and the rebels had some training camps on the other side. I was shown around the estates, and we spent the night in a ranger's house. The house was enclosed by high wire fencing, which was electrified by night, to discourage attack, and one had to carry a weapon at all times, even going to the loo! Nothing eventful happened that evening, with the three minders making it clear that they thought the trip was a waste of time. On our way back, about three kilometres from the house, coming down a steep hill, there was a tremendous blast. The Land Rover had been hit by a bomb placed in the road, which was cleverly covered over with a black bin bag, making it seem like tarmac. As the vehicle was protected from just such an eventuality, with five centimetres thick steel under the cab, and roll-over bars, it just heaved and rolled over. We quickly got out of our four-point seatbelts, waiting for the firing to start. All was quiet. After a few minutes, one of the guards cautiously crawled out the window, and when there was no reaction, we all got out, carefully looking for the ambush. The bomb was luckily, a one-off that had been placed after we had gone through the previous day, and the rebels had not bothered to hang around. We breathed a sigh of relief, but had to get the Land Rover on its wheels again and get out of there as quick as possible. It took an hour of sweating to get the winch rigged up around a suitably angled tree to get it righted, with two armed guards keeping careful watch some distance away for unwelcome visitors. All went well, with no further incidents, and we were in Umtali just after lunch.

The next cog in the wheels to get in motion was the permit for hauling the wattle by train to the Mozambique coast at Beira, along a slow narrow-gauge railway. In the meantime, waiting for what I thought was to be a routine export permit – as the government badly needed the foreign exchange - I took a trip to N. Carolina to see the equipment. I was very impressed by the system and we agreed a price. It now needed only a few details to be ironed out in Rhodesia to get things moving. I did not understand the Rhodesian Railways quota system for trains. Their letter of approval came back and I was awarded 9 out of 10 in priority ratings; way down the list. I was told by all there that there was very little or no chance of getting any charcoal exported by rail. That very quickly brought a full stop to any charcoal enterprise. Several months of work, at considerable cost, all for nothing!

I had a cousin, a Catholic priest, who was at a mission school near the Mozambique border, so I made a trip to see him. I finally found the mission late in the evening, and it was dark when I pulled into the compound, near Rusape. The school was alongside, where the children boarded. There was great excitement at the arrival of a strange car at night, and all the kids were out of bed and clambering around. My cousin came out of a house; candle in hand, to see what the commotion was. After many greetings, we retreated to his place for a beer or two. We talked all night, with him telling me of the life there, the children in school, with many of their parents over the mountains in Mozambique, training to fight the Smith regime, or in hiding from the Rhodesian army. He brought some of the children on regular trips to see their parents in those camps. Eventually the Smith regime deported him, and he was later invited to return by Mugabe, and went back, after independence.

A year or so after his return to Zimbabwe, his mother was going to visit him, and wrote asking him if he needed her to bring anything for him. The reply came back by return of post – he wanted a chain-saw! His poor little seventy-five year old mother bought him a chain-saw; put it in her big suitcase, taking it all the way to Zimbabwe, through Dublin and London airports, arriving without a bother, at the mission station in the eastern highlands. The mind boggles; if it were after the World Trade Centre disaster, she would have police and security from everywhere all asking her the same question; "madam, just exactly do you intend to do with this chain-saw"?

Near Rusape were some amazing standing stones, most weighting many tons, doing incredible balancing acts, one on the other. A young local boy asked me if I would like to see some rock carvings, and brought me to see them in a small cave. Hopefully, the government has made some effort to protect their ancient heritage.

Despite petrol rationing, I made a side trip back to Umtali to see a priest who came from a few kilometres of my home in Donegal. I knew his uncle, Frank, and thought it would be of interest to the priest to speak to a local of his father's family. I should have saved my breath, and petrol. I had woken him from his siesta, and he was not in the least interested in hearing about his poor relation. I soon bade him goodbye, and checked into the only hotel in town. There I learned that 'standards' were all important! In the restaurant, I was politely advised that I could not be served, as I was incorrectly dressed, I had to wear a tie. I had none with me, and asked for one at the front desk, only to be told that they did not do such things. The German manager was equally haughty, advising me that I could have a sandwich in my room. There was nowhere else to eat in the small town, and security made it imprudent to venture into the 'citi' – the African enclave. I went back to the priest's house. There I gave him a story, got a clerical collar from him, and went back to the restaurant, and was served without to-do, and with bowing and scraping, and grovelling apologies, as they had not been aware that I was a priest! While there is a will, there is a way!

Chapter 13

Rocket base set-up ??

I made several successful trips to Zambia, playing close to the wind, sniffing at danger, and enjoying the intrigue of 'beating the system' by smuggling both ivory and money out of the country with a fair degree of success. My special s...t detector was beginning to work overtime again. Having had a very good trip to Luangwa Valley National Park, I decided it was time for a change and to find new fields to research. I spent a few weeks in London waiting for a visa to Zaire. It was the only place I could get it, as it had to be applied for at the nearest embassy to my home. I lodged in the Irish Club in Eaton Square, sadly a club that exists no more. I was ready for my next voyage, wondering what it would bring me. Having heard of Lubumbashi, not far over the border in Zaire from Zambia, I thought that would be a good starting point, and if things did not work out, I could always go back over the border to Zambia. On my first visit to Zambia, I considered it an awful place, but that was relative to Europe.

I was in for a shock in Zaire. It is a total conundrum and one of the few African countries that have regressed since independence. It has all the wealth to be the greatest country on earth, with copper, diamonds, cobalt, gold and many precious or semi- precious commodities in abundance. Much of the heart of the country is dense jungle, with the minerals mainly to be found in the peripheries, with many of them in Katanga, now Shaba Province. It is bordered by Zambia, Angola, Congo (Congo Brazzaville), Central African Republic, Sudan, Uganda, Rwanda, Burundi, and Lake Tanganyika, and makes up a large part of the central African map, about one and a half million square kilometres. The Zaire River (now the Congo River) is one of the great African rivers, rising in Zambia, flowing north for one thousand five hundred kilometres, then west, before heading south to the sea near Matadi – the small land enclave of Zaire between Angola and Congo Brazzaville, a distance of some five thousand kilometres. Katanga alone is about the size of France, and the country as a whole about four times bigger than France, with a population of over sixty-five millions. They speak about two hundred languages, the most popular being Lingala, Chokwe, Songo, and Tschiluba, spoken by the Baluba tribe, of Katanga. It became the territory of King Leopold 2nd of Belgium from the Berlin Conference of 1884/85, which was engineered by King Leopold just for that purpose, as he wished to have a colony somewhere in Africa, and became known as the Belgian Congo. The Congolese finally got their independence in 1960, when the Belgians left the country within six months of an agreement to leave, when there were only two qualified African medical doctors for the whole of the country, and two thousand kilometres of tarmac road. Now, fifteen years after independence, there were considerably less tarmac roads.

This is where I landed myself now. In the 'heart of darkness' where another Irishman, Sir Roger Casement, wrote a report for the British Government, which finally put a stop to the slave trade there at the turn of the century. I had some experiences in Zambia and Rhodesia which acclimatised me to some of the African ways of doing things, but I was a total novice on reaching Lubumbashi, on how the country worked, and how things were done.

I was several days in the Park Hotel in Lubumbashi, in the town centre, finding my way around, checking things out, and at breakfast one morning, I met Peter, an Englishman, trying to order breakfast with his two words of French. He was typical of his race, many who never bothered to learn any foreign language, happy in the knowledge that English ruled the world, and Britannia was the world. On offering help, gratefully received, he informed me that he was a pilot with Otrag, a German company which had secured rights to set up a base to test orbital rockets for 'peaceful' purposes. He was one of a forward team which was looking for a suitable location, and with his German colleagues spent several weeks flying a small Dornier plane all over Shaba. President Mobutu had given them 100,000 square kilometres as their private domain. They took hundreds of photos, and eventually identified a location.

There was just one small problem! How to get on this site, which was on a 700 metres high plateau over a fast flowing river, with lots of scrub land, about 800 kilometres from the airport? The solution was obvious! Someone had to parachute in there to set up the base, and make a runway for the plane to land. That someone turned out to be Klaus, a smart, but half-mad Munchener, who had made lots of jumps in his pastime of skydiving. To drop alone was out of the question, so I was approached to go as a helper. Having never jumped before did not seem to be a problem to them, and I welcomed the adventure, so I was recruited.

I was given rudimentary instruction as to how to fall, and we were on our way to the plateau in the Argusy, an ex-British Air Force small cargo plane, with a maximum capacity of seven tons, with good short take- off and landing capabilities. There was over a ton of items needed for the setting up, including axes, machetes (the African answer to an all purpose big knife, about one metre long), food and water, tents, and enough whatever to last us several weeks without any further supplies. I was assured by Klaus that he would hold my hand when we were at the rear drop-down door of the Argusy, ready to jump when the pilot instructed. True to his word, he held my hand while the rear ramp opened and left us staring at bush thousands of metres below. The Indian pilot took us around in a slow circle, dropping as low as he dared, to enable us to jump. We were hooked on, all ready for the green light. Klaus stepped back swiftly, gave me the biggest kick in the arse I ever got, sending me literally flying. After a moment the jerk of the strap pulled me up short with the opening of the chute, and I drifted slowly to the earth – which was coming at a terrific speed to meet me. As in all the best movies, I touched down, rolled, and when I got my breath, picked myself up, only to see Klaus landing a few metres away, touching down like a true professional, on his two feet, as light as early morning gossamer on an Irish mountainside .

Ranjid, one of the pilots, could be a bit difficult at times. He was nicknamed Gunga-Din by his colleagues, and was an excellent pilot. It was a pleasure to be in the plane on landing, when he took the broad underbelly to within a metre of the runway, let the aircushion take effect, and land the plane as if on a crate of eggs. (Some twenty years later, in a bar in Brussels, this man approached me, asking if we had ever met before. It was Gunga-Din.)

The real work started then – with the plane slowly circling above, dropping small 'chutes with our supplies as near as possible to where we were. All went well for about thirty minutes until the water, which was in plastic containers, supported by airbags, came down. One by one, they exploded. The airbags were too light! We had a small problem. Stuck on a plateau without water was a death sentence! To go down to the river to drink was no better, as it was probably polluted. The crew had a bright idea! They had to leave as it was getting dark, and would come back the next morning with water. We were not in a position to argue, so set up out tents before nightfall, which comes very quickly, in about ten minutes, ready to settle in to an uncertain period of our lives, which could be very short lived at that point.

Next morning, having slept the sleep of the innocent, we were up bright and early with the sun, and after a breakfast of tinned fruit, started collecting the stores scattered over the bush. The parachutes would make shelter from the sun for the food. Not long into the morning we heard the drone of the plane coming back, and radio contact was swiftly made through our mobile unit, getting surprisingly long distance transmission, due to our elevation. They assured us that the problem had been solved, and sure enough, when they opened the ramp, dumped a load of containers with their little parachutes, cushioned with good strong airbags, all landed without problems. Assured, they then headed back to base, promising to come back every day. This pattern was repeated until they eventually landed on our make-shift strip.

We now had a small challenge – how to make a runway for this short take-off and landing plane in as short a time as possible! Once again, German thoroughness came to the fore. We set off, at intervals, multicoloured flares, which could be seen many kilometres away. Within a few days, local tribesmen gradually came to see what was going on at the uninhabited plateau. Gung-ho Klaus was all for getting them to work immediately. Unfortunately, they did not, for some unexplained reason, speak German or English, and did not understand his gesturing, which got even wilder as the poor locals were totally dumbfounded by this strange being. He then had a brainwave. He offered the chief of the group a can of sardines, making motions that it was really good to eat. The chief took the box, sniffed it, and promptly threw it away, as it did not have any smell. Klaus had only been in Africa for a few weeks at this time, and still had to absorb the fact that there were people who had never seen a white man, had never seen a tin can, nor eaten a white man's food. The whole group, by this time numbering about twenty, then did the same as the chief, scattering the food cans all over the place. I had to do something! Without making any fuss, I started to collect all the cans into a pile in front of the chief. When I had gathered as many as I could, I then split a tin of corned beef with my panga, and started to eat with my fingers, making appropriate noises as to the excellent quality of the food, and offered the other half of the tin to the chief. He tasted it, hesitantly, but after a minute, a great big smile crossed his scarred face, and he helped himself to the remainder of the can. A general scramble then ensured, with everyone diving for a tin or two, or more. When all had feasted, cutting themselves on the rough edges as they opened the tins with their pangas, (a smaller version of a machete), and things had calmed down, we got them to understand that they could have plenty to eat, but first they had to do a little work. They were promptly issued with axes, hoes, machetes and new pangas, through the chief, making him the giver of the precious items, and ensuring that he was beholden to us for the new-found wealth which befell all the Africans there. In no time, (African time, which meant when they were ready) all were at work cutting bushes and scrub along the major part of the plateau, clearing a swathe of more than 500 metres along the centre. In the meantime, more Africans were coming, alerted by the flares, and soon there were over one hundred men working away, with the result that in ten days, there was some semblance of a runway.

The plane, which meantime made a visit each day, came down really low, scaring the bejasus out of the workers, the pilot made a very low pass to inspect the landing strip, and decided it adequate for a landing. This was scheduled for the next day. The surprise and awe on the faces of the workers, seeing this big bird land, bumping along to a stop in clouds of dust, was a photo opportunity missed. The crew were Gods who could do no wrong – their wish was obeyed without question. Out of the body of the plane, down the ramp, came a small bulldozer driven by Gunga-Din, doing his little boy act, thoroughly enjoying himself. There were drums of diesel, with a generator for lighting. Trips from the base, almost two hours flying time from the plateau, were done on a daily basis, with a decent runway gradually taking shape.

Eventually, a Boeing 707 was able to land, direct from Munich, with all sorts of technical equipment. A special trip had to be made for each glass panel for the control tower, as they weighed two tons each. No customs control there! Mobutu had given them full control of over 100,000 square kilometres of territory as their own principality. The German Government did an equally generous gesture in giving the German investors 365 per cent tax deduction for investing in the project, something that prompted questions in the German Parliament later, with many articles in the international press. For the present, my job was done there, with the site operational.

ROCKET BASE SET-UP 77

ROCKET BASE SET-UP

Sometime later, after the first incursion of the Katanganese to Kolwezi in May 1977, I suggested to Klaus that he should look to getting proper security at the base, as they could be a target for insurgents, and a valuable target for ransom or worse. He put the idea to his company. They asked for a plan, which I gave them. I considered that ten trained men with sufficient weapons could secure the plateau against a small army, owing to the nature of the place, with steep cliffs falling to a fast flowing river some seven hundred metres below. They deemed it unnecessary, mainly because to the remoteness of the location, but by the second incursion of the Katanganese one year later, quickly changed their minds. Unfortunately, I had to decline their invitation, telling them that it would take up to four months to set up properly, and at which time it would be too late to take any avoiding action.

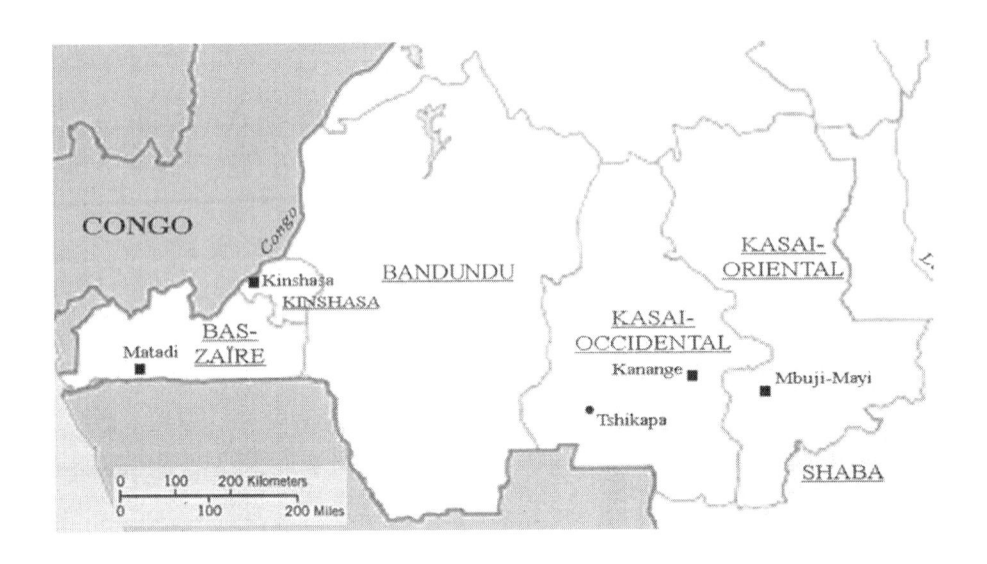

Chapter 14

Kolwesi 1

Going to Lubudi by train, one of the few remaining from the old Belgian pre 1960 regime was quite an experience. No problem about timekeeping a la Swiss! The trains left when they were good and ready, with no timetable, nor any urgency to get there that day or the next. Getting on the train was something else, with a line of soldiers and police, checking all passengers, and ripping them off for as much as they could – a national pastime. Obviously, a European travelling was a certainty for searching, and extracting what they could. They did better than expected from me, having dug into my bag and finding my cash at the bottom. It took a big lump of it to keep the security man quiet, before others got in on the act, with the possibility of losing all. We got a seat, and waiting with some anxiety, we finally moved off at a leisurely pace of about thirty kilometres per hour, rocking and swaying with the narrow gauge tracks, and hoping it would not be derailed. Various stops saw the whole village population along the track, shouting out their wares, selling anything they had, from greasy Manioc cooked in old oil, to great big cane rats, charcoaled, fully skinned and ready for eating, teeth still in situ! Monkey brains were, to the Africans, a delicacy, but I always firmly refused to eat it, and was later proved to be a serious contributor to a terrible disease. They were not the nicest presentation in the world, and doubt if they would pass muster in the George Cinque in Paris or any well known eatery in London or New York, but when hungry, it's amazing what one can eat.

Many hours later, we finally arrived at Likasi, the end of the line for me, and I settled in the guest house, to await my truck which was due in the next day or two, by previous arrangement with a dealer in Lubumbashi, to arrive from Kamina Base, the Zaire Air Force base in the north of Shaba. The base was built in order to keep the rebellious locals in line, and as an emergency landing strip for the American shuttle craft, in the event they had need to make emergency landings in the early days. Those emergency bases were gradually made redundant with the advances in technology, leaving Mobutu with a runway over three kilometres long, and were used only by a few fighter jets provided by the Belgians, who first made sure they were superfluous to their own requirements. Three days later, the truck arrived, with the driver proudly showing me all the equipment on it, and making sure that I appreciated his ingenuity in putting several drums of diesel in the back, as well as the long range feul tanks especially fitted. We settled the sale price, after the inevitable bargaining, without which any deal, big or small, is closed. The driver then took his leave to make his way back to the base, having made a nice payday from the truck, leaving the Zaire Air Force short one fine truck and some diesel.

Another two weeks of haggling, refusing, buying, sorting, and general messing about, (shades of an old-time Irish fair day) saw me with a decent mixed cargo of crocodile skins and ivory, and heading from Lukasu to Kolwesi en-route to Lubumbashi. One day's drive to Kolwesi, all going well, no hiccups, and well rested in the Impala Hotel, saw me on the way for the easiest part of the journey – only four hours drive on a reasonably good road all the way to Lubumbashi.

I headed off in great spirits, towards the airport at the eastern edge of town, fully happy to be on the last leg of what should have been a fruitful trip. There is a lesson to be learned every day. I should not have begun to count my chickens before all was secure. The roadblock at the airport turnoff did not put me at ease. A ragtag of men, armed to the teeth, had taken over the airport, and they were taking all they could from passing

KOLWESI 1

travellers. High on their list was transport, especially mine. They were grateful for my 'gift', and whatever I 'offered', leaving me with my boots, socks, jeans, and most importantly, my passport. My choices were then, I did not have any, except to walk back the five kilometres to town, hoping there was some good news there. There was none, as word was filtering back about the Katanganese rebels having returned from Angola. These were the same people who had departed during the U.N. interception in 1961, and had vowed revenge, while earning a living as security for DeBeers diamond mines in Angola.

(The U.N intervened during the Katanganese uprising, and was headed by an Irishman, Conor Cruise O'Brien. Fifteen years later, Katanganese who asked me my name, remembered him, thinking I was of the same 'tribe'. It did not take me long to realise that they were using the family name, rather than the Christian first name method, thereby mixing us up. I soon made it clear that I had nothing to do with O'Brien! Patrice Lumumba, the Katanganese Prime Minister, was executed with the help of the CIA and Belgium authorities at that time, and now they wanted revenge.)

I was holed up in the Impala Hotel, with a lot of Europeans who had gathered, trying to figure out what to do. Rumour was rife, panic not far away, but after two days, radio contact assured us that the Zaire army, with the crack troops of Mobuto's elite, were landing from Kamina Base, and routing the Katanganese rebels. Some faded away to their villages; others headed their way out of the country, with the rebels helping themselves to seventy truck loads of cobalt, a precious metal, for their resupply, taking it back to Angola. The shortage of cobalt on the world market then put the price skyrocketing, getting a much better price for the Katanganese than they had anticipated. With all that cash, they were able to retrain and rearm, coming back the following year – but that is another story. I was eventually able to get a lift with a Belgian to Lubumbashi.

I was staying in the Park Hotel in the town centre, helping out a little with the Otrag crew with all wondering what was the news, with a lot of rumours going around, as usual in such situations. We did not have long to wait. On the second night in the hotel, about four o'clock in the morning, there was an almighty kick on my door, with shouts along the corridor of 'all out'. On opening the door to see what the commotion was about, I was ᴊ at that all had to get to the airport as soon as possible. I did not ᴊ any more encouragement, but put my things in a plastic bag (razor, ᴊwel, and some soap, along with two T shirts that the crew had given me) and we all four were on our way to the airport within fifteen minutes. The captain had got word that the Zaire army wanted to commandeer the plane, and his instructions were not to let that happen, if at all possible. We got to the plane, all got in, getting ready for take-off, with me being instructed to secure any boxes or anything that could move, in the belly of the plane. The four engines were revving up to full pitch, and I did not hear the shout to fasten-up. The Argusy suddenly took off along the runway like a greyhound from a trap, with me holding on for dear life to some strops.

I could see in the first light that trucks were being driven on the runway, trying to stop our take-off, but they had not realised the very short take-off capability of the Argusy. The plane tail must have been only centimetres from scraping on the runway, such was the steep ascent. We were airborne in just over one hundred metres, with the trucks left idling there, growing smaller as we gained height. We could now see that they were indeed, Zaire army trucks. It had been a close call! The pilot set a course for Kananga to refuel, as we did not have the range to go all the way to Kinshasa in one go.

There were no satellite navigation systems then, other than those controlled by the U.S. military, and direction was calculated by the navigator and dead reckoning. This made some trips interesting, due to the plane not being pressurised, limiting our normal ceiling height to about four and a half thousand metres. With many tropical storms building up, it was often necessary to fly around the cumulus rather than risk the turbulence going through them, and it was like flying in the Grand Canyon, looping left and right, descending and climbing in trying to get a clear path through the clouds. I was thrilled watching lightening on either side of the plane, making its jagged way to earth, where it often hit a giant tree, exploding the tree in a huge flame, and starting forest fires.

We refuelled at Kananga without incident, and next stop was Kinshasa. I landed there absolutely stony broke, and with not a clue as to which way to turn.

Chapter 15

Michel after Kolwesi/-Kisangani

I first met him at the bar of the Park Hotel, Lubumbashi, where he spoke to me in reasonable English. He was a Baluba, about thirty-five years of age (I always found it difficult to guess the age of Africans, and often under-estimated). He was well dressed, in 'European' attire, and seemed to be a very friendly person – which he was, as I found out. He was a local, but lived mainly in Kinshasa, where he had a wife and three children in the affluent area of Gombe. His wife was a diplomat, but I never found out exactly where she worked, except that she seemed to have many good contacts.

Michel was a businessman, which can mean many things in Zaire, but obviously, he was fairly successful. We got on very well and met again a few days later. Over a few beers, we discussed many things, and he gave me much good advice. One thing that struck me about him, that unlike many Africans, he never asked for money, or took advantage in any way. Quite the contrary, he helped me stay out of harm's way, guiding me from insincere people, and bad deals. He refused to wear the Mobutu suit which the President wore, and was worn by many as a lean towards the almighty President, a kind of uniform not unlike the Chinese traditional suit worn by millions under Chairman Mao. His was not deferent to Mobutu, rather mocked him, but was careful about ears in the vicinity when he spoke disparagingly about 'plan Mobutu' – the locals' way of making fun of Mobutu Sese Soko's dictates. We met after he had gone to Kinshasa, each time I visited there, as the bar at the Intercontinental Hotel was on his stamping ground list.

The top floor of the hotel had a very nice restaurant, where I eat on several occasions as well as in any European fine diner, and had a first-class orchestra playing a mixture of African and international music. It was there that the Maitre d' made excellent Irish coffee, with a great play to the details of warming the glass on a Bunsen burner, and going through the whole process. The view through the floor to ceiling windows was mesmerising, overlooking the whole city, and across the river Congo to Brazzaville, the capital of the Republic of Congo, as distinct from the Democratic Republic of Congo (Zaire), and is often referred to as Congo-Brazza. It is an ex-French colony, and unlike Zaire, one could leave a purse or handbag on a café table, returning some time later, to find it still there, intact. This was achieved by the simple and effective rule that thieves had their right hands chopped off. That all changed with the civil unrest of the '90's.

Mobutu was President (Joseph Desire Mobutu Sese Seko Nkuku Ngbendu wa Za Banga – the almighty one, etc.) from 1965 to 1997 when he went into exile, and died of cancer in Morocco some time later. It is estimated that he had stolen over four billion U.S. dollars from Zaire, buying at least eight chateaux in France, six in Belgium, built a palace that has been described as Zaire's Versailles at Gdadlite, his home village, where he built an international airport, with a six lane motorway leading four kilometres to his palace. The palace alone cost over twenty million U.S. dollars. All has now been recovered by jungle. I later met an Englishman in Kinshasa who was at his wits end trying to get export permits for the heavy equipment used in the airport construction. Wimpey's had the contract, all the permits for importing the necessary equipment, but none for export.

After the May 1977 Kolwesi invasion by the Katanganese who came back from Angola, I arrived in Kinshasa and tried to raise some funds to continue my expeditions. I had met Tony the Belgian, from Liege, once or twice, and approached him for a loan He advanced me what I thought necessary, at extortionist rates. I was flush again! I knew there was plenty of ivory to be had in the Equator province, near the borders of the Central African Republic, so I headed for Kisangani on the first available flight, which was in three days time, and only managed to get there with the expediency of a little 'matabisch', the Zaire equivalent of European brown envelopes. There was a little kafuffle at the airport, where a woman claimed she had a confirmed seat, mine, but she was finally persuaded to wait for the next flight, whenever that would be. The plane to Kisangani was on a round trip via Bunia, Bukavu, Lubumbashi, and back to Kinshasa – possibly a trip of up to four days. Presumably she would have slept on the floor in the airport main hall waiting for the plane's return. It was not unusual to have up to one hundred people sleeping there, all waiting for their planes. The trip was uneventful for the most part, until we arrived near to Kisangani, where the turbulence was quite bad. The tropical storm was so bad that we were tossed about quite a bit, with some of the passengers on the floor, holding on for dear life to any solid object, moaning that the end of the world had come. We finally circled the new airport several times, trying to land. I was sure the pilot would tell us it was not possible, and that we had to go to Bunia, but on the third approach, he was able to land. Just how he did it in such a storm left me in admiration, as I'm sure had the same happened in Europe, there would be no question of the plane landing. The Boeing 737 was rocked back and forth on the runway with the force of the gale, and we had to wait forty-five minutes for it to abate enough to allow the crew to open the doors. Meantime, the temperature in the cabin had soared to a very uncomfortably hot and humid level, making everyone short tempered. That was resolved as the door was opened. The temperature outside was over 40 Centigrade, and a humidity of 100 per cent, made the evening a little uncomfortable. When the storm cleared an hour or so later, I was able to get a taxi to the other side of town to Simi-Simi, to my base at the Catholic Mission, where they gave me my usual room.

Next trick; to business, to earn the money lent to me, and to make as much as possible as soon as possible! Needs must; I had to replenish the coffers! As luck would have it, on contacting one or two whom I knew in town, there was word of a substantial hoard of ivory deep in the forest by a certain village. A deal was done with the Mission to hire their Land Rover, which we stocked up with the usual lot of bottled water, tins of pilchards and corned beef, some crates of beer, and enough bread to last a few days before it went off completely. A few kilos of smoked deer biltong were a good standby, which would keep us going for a week by chewing it slowly. This was made by a local Greek who lived entirely off his own resources on his smallholding on the edge of town.

Finally we were on our way, heading north for two days, staying in village huts along the way, sharing the usual news, with a few beers to the local chief, before turning in early – it was dark a little after six o'clock. Having sat around the fire for a few hours, with everything gradually getting quiet from the birds and animals, settling in with only the night noises from some nocturnal animals and birds to break the deafening silence, and the whole village bedded down. At sun-up, about five o'clock, the village gradually came to life, and we were soon on our way, until we turned off the main track, heading west. The track gradually got worse, until there was only a walking track visible. My guide had to sit on the roof of the cab, to direct me. I was crawling along in second gear, ready to stop anytime he saw a fallen tree across the path. Those stops were a relief to me, giving me a chance to descend to a little fresh air, as the windows had to be closed owing to the pollen from the elephant grass which threatened to smother me. I had tried several times to open the window a little for air, as the temperature in the cab was stifling, but it was impossible to continue, so the respites were very welcome. It was then a job for the winch on front to try to haul the fallen tree out of the way, sometimes with the help of our big Tirfor, a big hand-operated winch which was anchored to a tree and then winched slowly by pumping the handle on the return cable, and using the axe, chopping branches to ease the path. We were heading north-west, into dry forest land, so luckily did not have to contend with swamp lands as well. Several times we hit tree trunks that the lookout did not see, but some of them were rapidly going back to compost, and were relatively easy to remove.

One massive, recently fallen tree trunk completely barred our way, and with the best efforts, took us two days to chop and remove. During one of my respites from chopping, with my African doing a great job, I noticed a green Mamba near his head, just moving ever so slowly towards him. To shout would probably scare him, and induce the Mamba to drop on him, where the poison from its bite would have been fatal in about twenty minutes. A casual wave to him to come to me worked wonders, and when I pointed out the snake, he made quick work of it with his panga, cutting its head off. We had delicious fresh meat for our barbeque that evening, having done a fine job of slitting it open, cleaning it out and skinning it – shades of my school days snaring rabbits and skinning them, saving the fur complete. Taking turns on the axe and pulling with the winch was hard work; until towards the end of the second day, the track was clear enough to allow us to squeeze though. It took only one more day to reach the village, where we went through the usual greetings with the chief, sharing a beer, and shooting the bull.

We were the first vehicle traffic to penetrate that far in many years, and the children had never seen a white man. That was always a thing of wonder to them, as they could not figure out why my skin was different from theirs.

It took a lot of persuasion on the part of my African to convince the chief that I was not Belgian, and that I was willing to buy ivory at a decent price, without cheating them. Finally, the next day, the chief brought us a few small ivory tusks. They were not of good quality, and obviously had been buried for some considerable time, and were beginning to decompose. Much as I would have liked to reject them out of hand, we had to go through the motions of bargaining, and after several hours, agreed on an inflated price. The options were to make a deal for that lot, and then the real hoard would be produced, or we would leave empty handed. The second option was a non-starter, after the trouble of getting there; six days of clearing the track, so the deal was done. The chief and a few village 'wise men' were happy, so we turned in that evening, having dined at the chief's invitation, on chicken and Irish potatoes.

By noon the next day we were bid to go to the chief's house. There he had good sized tusks laid out for our inspection. These again had been buried, but were in pristine condition, weighting about six kilograms average. The forest elephant does not have tusks as big as those of the savannah, owing to a different diet, but these were as good as one could expect there. The usual haggling began again, reminding of an old fair day in my home area, where a cow was sold after much to-ing and fro-ing , walking away, holding out of hands, spitting on them and finally, an agreement of how much good-luck money would go back to the buyer. It took most of the afternoon, with a lot of rejecting of offers between the few 'wise men' in the hut. We had to be careful not to insult them by offering too little, but also to get the tusks at a reasonable price, without paying ridiculous 'white man' prices. Finally a deal was done, the ivory was weighted on our portable scales as well as on the village scales, which were a simple balance of several stones used uniquely for that purpose. We were just finished, having a little drink of the local potent stuff, made from fermented coconut, which could almost blow ones head off, when there was great commotion outside.

A rogue elephant had once again, gone through the local vegetable garden, cleaning it out, leaving a total mess behind. The villagers had tried several times to capture him, without avail, so we were corralled into agreeing to go on the hunt the following morning. It was an honour to be asked, and we could not refuse. It was agreed that we should head off at first light, with a group of six, four stalkers and two helpers for the food etc., as we might be a few days on the trip. The only weapons that they had available were poison spears and bows and arrows. Unless the poison was very potent, it would be a tough nut to crack.

I worked late at the 4x4 getting my old AR180, (a high velocity rifle smuggled in from Swaziland, where there was a glut of Eastern produced rifles) out of its box which was welded into the jeep, as part of the furniture, sufficient to be overlooked by most at casual inspection. It had to be cleaned, assembled, and checked for any problems, with a few rounds 'doctored' as dum-dums for greater effect, before heading off in the morning. It was something that was not normally used, only for cases of extreme emergency, but I figured that the lives of the village were at stake by this rogue, deeming it necessary.

We headed off shortly after dawn, amid many good wishes from all at the village, into the dense forest in the direction they knew the rogue to go. All day long, trekking, stopping whilst the scouts checked the routes taken, sometimes doubling back, until after the fourth day, we had a definite sighting of it in some dense bush. Amazingly, a big elephant can be almost invisible in the forest, until one is within metres of him, and then maybe too late to make a discreet retreat. It took us two hours to circle the elephant, getting slightly to the rear of it, and I was set up for a good shot. That was all it took, one behind the right ear upwards into the head, and he dropped silently like a stone. There was great rejoicing, and the drum of the hunters sounded out the news, to be answered shortly by the Tam-Tam of the village much deeper thundering sound. Each village knew their own Tam-Tam sound, and the invitation went out to the feast.

The hunters were busy cutting the ivory tusks, about five kilograms each, and stripping the meat from the best parts of the carcass. Another was busy getting a big fire going nearby, and as dark descended, nearly all the village arrived to much shouting and laughter. I did not have a camera, but it would have been a precious sight to record about six Africans eating freshly grilled meat, all from the biggest spare rib I ever saw. There was much hilarity and partying until late, with everyone eventually bedding down by the fire, which was a must by now to discourage the animals from the smell of meat. Early next morning, everyone took as much as they could carry in their tin dishes on their heads, or tied by banana string, back to the village, leaving the rest of the feasting to the vultures and wild animals to clean the forest again, as is nature's way. Back at the village, we quickly prepared to take our departure. I was greatly honoured when the chief, with much gesturing, presented me with the bigger of the two tusks from the rogue elephant as appreciation in my part. (Elephant tusks are never the same size, as they forage with the left tusk, making it slightly shorter).

I did not want to hang around now that they knew that I had a good rifle. The 4x4 was loaded, the money passed over, and very soon we were on our return journey, which took us only two days to reach the Mission base.

I was now with approximately 500 kilograms of fine tusks – good dark ivory with a hint of pink towards the base – a result of their excellent diet (and especially this one, having plundered several village gardens), enough to get to Antwerp, pay my debts, and a little left over to begin again. The Brother at the Mission, with the approval of the Head, made me a few fine boxes to transport the ivory. All was packed as tightly as possible, and brought to the airport for freighting to Kinshasa, en route to Paris. During the time I waited to have the boxes made, I overheard the priests speak of the news on their radio network. A priest had gone deep into the forest and baptised the whole village I had left some days previously. None had been there in over twelve years, but some European had cleared the route! I felt the priest had taken advantage of my hard work, but maybe God works in mysterious ways.

(The Mission base had regular daily radio contact with all their outlaying stations, each station reporting back in turn.)

Brussels airport was never used as a destination base, I do not know why, but it was avoided like the plague for such transactions – just too much trouble. I had no worries about the shipment internationally, as by now I had a legal permit to trade ivory (don't ask how that was done, something to do with brown envelopes). All went well; I arrived in Kinshasa on the same plane as the ivory, and went to the Intercontinental Hotel to arrange my trip the next day.

Things did not go quite to plan, as the next morning, Michel came into the lobby with a scruffy-looking man. I wondered what he was doing with such a person, when they both came over, and Michel indicated that we take a seat. He began to explain to me, in English, that the scruffy individual was a special cop, and was looking for me. Obviously the cop did not know what I looked like. Michel quietly asked me to casually make my way to his car which was outside, and he would join me in a few minutes, which he did. We were just pulling away when the cop blocked our way, and stuck his pistol at me. I was under arrest! I did not know what for, but we were on our way to prison. There I was stripped of any money, my watch, passport, and shown to a cell. I had visions of being there for months, with no way of getting out! My cell was shared with an ex-governor of Lubumbashi who was, he told me, there for embezzlement. The door was left open, and one could wander outside at will in the big open space. This was a hive of activity, with whole families gathering around, children playing, some women cooking on little fires, and with a general festival air about the place, seemed not too bad. There are no meal times there, as the prisoners are only fed by their own families or friends on the outside. Luckily Michel came to my rescue, bringing me a decent meal about five o'clock in the evening. The next day was going to be a long one! No place to go, nothing to do, and all day to worry about it. About two o'clock in the afternoon, a guard came and brought me to the office near the entrance gate, where he brought out an envelope with all my belongings, even my watch and money, had me sign for it, and I was free. Outside, Michel was waiting to bring me to the hotel, and on the way, began to explain what had happened, and why I was arrested.

The ivory had been 'misplaced' by the French pilot of the 737 from Kisangani to Kinshasa, and scheduled for shipping to Paris by UTA. Tony, my backer, who was a pilot, had been at the airport, and found out what was happening. He put two and two together and came to the wrong conclusion, thinking that I was trying to hoodwink him of his money. He then used his influence to teach me a lesson. Luckily, my good friend Michel had started checking through his own sources, and between him and Tony, found out that the Frenchman was simply stealing my cargo. The cargo was commandeered at the airport, the Frenchman went into hiding, and I was let free. Problem solved! Much later I heard that Tony was not the only person looking for the thief, and that he escaped and made his way to France, by taking the ferry to Brazzaville, just across the river from Kinshasa, and the capital of the Republic of Congo (Brazzaville).

The way now opened for my trip to Antwerp, via Paris. This time there were no panic stations, and a few days after landing in Paris, the consignment arrived at the 'Natural' warehouse where my contact, Willy, and I weighed the ivory, agreed a price, he paid out, and I was all set to begin my life again.

CENTRAL AFRICAN REPUBLIC
Gemena
Aketi
Lisala
Bumba
Congo
Congo
CONGO
EQUATEUR
0 100 200 Kilometers
0 100 200 Miles

Chapter 16

Foiled hi-jacking attempt '77

We had been out over a week or so from the Kisangani base, looking for ivory, and having come up against a brick wall in that respect, we decided to head back to base. We had plenty of diesel, time was no problem, so we headed back early one morning on the 500 kilometre-odd journey from near Gemena, in the Bangala region, not far from Bangui, the capitol of the Central African Republic. The road, in Zaire terms, was quite good, and we made good time, speeding along at a good pace of about 30 kilometres per hour. All went well for several hours until we reached the crossing of the Mongala River, which feeds into the Congo River a little further west. The ferry was on our side, waiting to do the crossing, and after a wait of an hour or two, we embarked, advancing slowly on to the ferry ramp. It was at this point that my side-kick guardian, a pigmy who came from the swamp area a few days trek west, decided that it was fine for me to travel alone, while he took advantage of the proximity to pay a visit to his village.

I had no problem with that, as the road on the other side was good as far as Lisala, where I had to cross the Congo River. We parted company, after his assurances that he would be in Kisangani in a few weeks, to continue his normal duties as guardian at the Mission base. I wished him well, and waved him goodbye, watched as he took up his usual lope, half running, at a good pace. He could keep up that pace all day, without visibly tiring. My last sight of him was as he disappeared into the forest, looking back and waving, in his loin cloth, with his quiver for his arrows and his little bow slung over his shoulder, with his food for a day or two tied in a little ball to his waist in a banana leaf.

I went on my way after shooting the bull as much as linguistically possible with the village chief on disembarking from the ferry, with ne'er a care, looking forward to a quiet trip all the way. I stopped for an old man and his wife who were on the road, waving me down for a lift, in the traditional fashion, arm outstretched, waving it up and down, and after indicating to them that they were to bang on the roof of the cab when they wanted off, helped them into the back of the pickup. I stopped once to make sure they still wanted to continue, afraid that they had misunderstood, and I had taken them many kilometres past their destination. They indicated that they were still heading in the right direction, so off we went again, only to be stopped at an army roadblock, set up to catch smugglers from Bangui, or rebels who were quite numerous in the area, not being very happy with the Mobutu regime. The soldiers asked the old couple if I was charging them for the lift, a common occurrence in Africa, where there was a set rate for each kilometre covered, which was, I think, one Makuta, or one percent of the local currency, the Zaire. They assured the soldiers that I had not asked for money, and after giving me a strange look, the soldiers sent me on my way. I was congratulating myself on the easy escape, whereas if I had charged the old couple, the army would have taken that and a lot more. One good deed....! It was near Bumba, after a distance of over 200 kilometres that the hammering on the roof stopped me. They had gone all that way to visit God knows what! It never ceased to amaze me the distances they travel, sometimes spending days on the road, sleeping where they find themselves. They were generous in their thanks, with much bowing and clasping of one hand on to the other, and I was on my way to Bumba, where I found the hostel in the village. I had a reasonable meal, a few cold beers, and a bed for the night.

Next morning, after a breakfast of good coffee and some bread hot from the bakery next door, I was on my way. I had only about twenty kilometres to go for the next ferry, crossing a tributary of the Congo on a small ferry capable of taking no more than four cars, and then it was heading for the crossing of the Congo at Basoke.

Not long after the crossing, I came to another army checkpoint. I was relaxed about it, having a pleasant surprise earlier. They could not believe their luck! A European, travelling alone, with a fine Toyota 4x4! After some questions, it was clear and they did not hide it, that they were a renegade army group, who were planning to plunder some nearby village. They had obviously been there for some days, judging by the camp fires and debris lying around. They were civil enough, telling me that the 4x4 would be a big plus for them when they made their raid on the village, and as they knew I could not go anywhere, they let me wander about freely, with the exception of going too close to the 4x4. I did not let them know that I was not in favour of them taking my jeep, leaving me with a two hundred kilometre walk back to Kisangani, along tracks through some of the most dense jungle in the world, where one would be lost after twenty metres in the permanent semi-darkness, with trees sprouting from treetops, up to three levels, over one hundred metres tall. That was one reason why I liked travelling with 'my' pigmy, although if he had been with me, I have no doubt that they would have killed him immediately. He could vanish in a flash, hidden by a branch, or up a tree, being totally invisible, and deadly with his bow and poisoned arrows. The only thing to do was to play along with them, to see what happened. With that in mind (and I did not have much of a choice – either that or they would take the jeep anyway), I settled in with them, asking questions as to their weapons, which part they were from, and generally making small talk. They fed me as one of themselves, and as darkness came, bade me to bed down near the fire, a prime location. Next morning was no different. They did not seem in any hurry to go anywhere, and so the day passed uneventfully. I had plenty of time to figure out a plan, such as it was, to hijack my jeep back and leave. By day two I was like one of them, and I think they trusted me a little; in so much as they gave me a demonstration of their heavy machine gun and their Swedish Gustav – a heavy old machine gun, but in good working condition. Before dawn on day three was to be my chance! I was awake nearly all night, watching the movements of the men around me, until all were fast asleep. Dawn comes early there, shortly after five o'clock, so I had to have the timing right to make my move. I quietly rose about an hour before that, going for a 'comfort stop', and waited a good fifteen minutes to get my night vision, before slowly making my way to the track, and back along it to the camp. That way, there was much less chance of treading on a twig, and waking a soldier. All went well; I crept up to the jeep, and eased myself into the cab via the open window, not daring to open the door in case the noise would alert them. The keys were, as I knew, still in the starter lock. Now was the tricky bit! I had to get the engine started, and the truck moving as fast as I could, otherwise I would be vulture meat. I turned on the motor, it started immediately, I rammed it into gear, gunned the accelerator, and was off like a harpoon from a whaling boat. Too bad about the soldier who was sleeping in the back! He jumped up, but with the forward momentum, fell off on to the track. I did not bother to look back, but kept my head down, expecting bullets to slam into my back every second, until there was a slight bend in the track, and I was safe.

Basoko was about an hour away, crossing the Congo on a small ferry, and I was envisaging the lot being swept down river if the flimsy-looking cable which guided the ferry and restrained it from going with the flow of about seven knots, suddenly snapped under the strain. It was only then that I began to relax a little, but still wondered about the village and its fate. Many African villages have a population of about 80 to 100 persons.

The next stretch of track was in very poor condition, necessitating four-wheel-drive most of the way, slowing the pace to no more than a tiring eight to nine kilometres per hour, where I finally reached Isangi as dark was falling, and after the usual visit to the local chief, I slept in the cab of the jeep. It was not the most restful of sleeps, but there is something about the 'rive gauche' that gave me a few anxious moments. There was tenseness in the air, nothing that one could explain, but just a strong feeling. Many men and women with reason to avoid the police, for example, sense police when they are near. There is no explaining the sensation. My sixth sense, which a New York friend described as my 's...t' detector, was on high alert, and I was glad to have a space on the ferry early in the morning, crossing the mighty Congo once more, to a spot near Yangambi, where there once was a thriving university, constructed by the Belgians just before independence, and now was in total ruins, plundered of everything that could be taken. From there to Kisangani was only two hours on a decent road, and a good shower by the banana tree plantation behind the school at the Mission. The mechanic at the Mission had a good look over the Land Rover. There were a few cracks in the chassis, which he had to weld, but the big bugbear with that model had not struck during that trip. I had previously broken several half-shafts, and always carried a spare, along with a brush handle to knock out the broken bit, before replacing the new shaft.

On telling the people at the Mission of my uneasy feeling on the 'rive gauche' they agreed with me. After all, they had lost thirty-one nuns and priests in that area during the Simba uprising in 1964, all being decapitated.

Chapter 17

Leaving for Canada Dec '77

I had met Jack on a trip to Kinshasa from my base in Kisangani. He had just arrived from Canada, along with four other pilots, and was hanging about waiting for their flight which would take them to Toronto, eventually. I got talking to them at the bar, but they seemed a bit reluctant to speak, directed me to their 'leader', Jack. He turned out to be a very open, friendly, likeable guy, who explained that they had just delivered a few Canada Air Electra CL44 planes, taking time off from their jobs to do a little out of the ordinary. The Electras were high swing-tail flying transporters which could carry a load of about twenty-seven tons long distances - ideal for Zaire. Jack appreciated my explanation of how to make phone calls to his home, without having to pay a fortune – about 250 U.S. dollars for a few minutes connection. All he had to do was call the switchboard from his room, getting the operator's name, and asking for the connection to be put on the 'system'. One normally got connected within a very few minutes, rather than having to wait hours, and sometimes days, to get a line. About ten minutes after finishing the call, there would be a discreet knock on the room door, and an envelope passed for the operator, who in turn took care of the international operator who made the whole thing possible. Such was the corruption in Zaire that it penetrated to all facets of society.

During a visit I made to the office of the Minister responsible for Post and Communications, (while asking for a radio permit for the proposed diamond buying base in Tshikapa) on a Friday afternoon, he phoned downstairs asking them in the main post office below. He ordered them to bring him the day's takings. A few minutes later, two men entered carrying a big metal box, of the kind one sees all over Africa. They swung open the lid, and left the office. It was 80 per cent full of all denominations of Zaires, the currency of the country. Apparently it was a regular happening, this being his pin money for the week-end?

Jack and I got on friendly terms over a few beers, and parted, exchanging names and addresses. I went back to the equator line, to Kisangani, to my base at Simi-Simi, where every time I disembarked from the plane there, it felt like a full face fist from a pro boxer, such was the heat, compared with relatively cool Kinshasa. It never took me long to get used to it, and indeed, I loved the heat.

There was a passenger ferry from Kinshasa to Kisangani which took twelve days to make the trip, with the return trip downriver taking only ten days. One could opt for steerage class, where no food was provided, at a very cheap price. It meant sleeping on any clear spot possible, and was very basic. Fifth class was quite decent with a small cabin, mostly used by Europeans who had a lot of baggage to transport, or well-off Africans, and reasonable food was provided, mostly fish, Capitan, a wonderful large fish from the river. Arriving at Kisangani was like a Mississippi river boat of a century ago, with tremendous hustle and bustle, music blaring from loudspeakers, with hundreds of people moving about, and everyone shouting above the noise.

Six months later, getting a bit restless with my travels east and west along the equator line from Kisangani, I began thinking of getting out of there for a while, before going 'native', as had happened with a lot of the Flemish, Greeks, and the occasional Italian still left there from the colonial days.

LEAVING FOR CANADA DEC '77

LEAVING FOR CANADA DEC '77

Wondering where to go, I came across Jack's name, thought that his invitation to visit might make a nice change from the heat and humidity, and gave him a call from the post office in the centre of town. It was one of the few 'modern' buildings, having just been finished before independence, and was still functioning. Alongside it was a lovely fountain, big as an Olympic swimming pool. The pool was used for a bit more practical purpose during the Simba uprising of 1964, when thousands were thrown over the falls, and thousands more decapitated, with their heads filling the fountain.

However, these were quieter times, and in no time at all, I had a connection. Would I be welcome if I took him up on his offer to stay in his home in Canada? There was no hesitation – of course I would! Would I be welcome at Christmas? He and his family would be delighted!

That was that, and so I made my plans. Tickets were booked. TAP, the Portuguese National Airline, would be my transporter for the trip, being the cheapest, as well as giving me an overnight in Lisbon at TAP expense. I had used this system many times on trips, deliberately timing my flights, ensuring that my trip could not be completed the same day. By my choosing a late flight where there could not be an immediate ongoing connection, gave me some 'tourist' time in some city. TAP assured me they would have a representative at Lisbon airport to meet me, to give me vouchers for a taxi and hotel, waiting for my ongoing flight to Toronto next afternoon.

Arriving at Lisbon airport at three a.m., there was no representative, and after going all over the airport, through non-existing custom zones, criss-crossing everywhere looking for the representative it was clear that they had not bothered, as one customer at three a.m. was no big priority.

Going through customs at seven o'clock was another affair. They had just started work, and one vigilant sod, seeing me casually going out of the custom area, again, abruptly called me to task. No amount of explaining would satisfy him – I had to open my suitcase. He had a good look through it, and then told me not to move, went off to another part of the building, coming back five minutes later with a mighty big screwdriver. He intimated that he was to tear the lining of my case. I was adamant that he was not. Standoff! That was quickly resolved when he marched me, bags and all, to a small room, locking the door on his way out. Two hours later, a more human looking man arrived who spoke good English. He had a man on tow who was going to slit the seams of the suitcase lining, to see what was in the space at the bottom. I told him not to bother, as I could do the necessary without all that palava. Emptying the case, I proceeded to undo the Velcro seams, well hidden by the lining beading, and reveal the two centimetre space at the bottom – empty! A few questions as to why I had it – smuggling drugs, diamonds? and on being told of the dangers of travelling in Africa with a large sum of cash, they seemed convinced, and let me go. I picked up my two bags; the suitcase, and my canary yellow hold-all, and recommenced my search for the elusive representative. The airport was buzzing at this time, nearly 10 o'clock, and the TAP desk quickly arranged the necessary vouchers, after my giving them the benefit of my temper.

(The suitcase had been bought in Antwerp near the Tourist Hotel, by the main rail station. An old gent fronted the bag shop, and on indicating my interest, showed me his handi-work, one of which I ordered, and picked up a week later, as it had to be made to order at a cost of six hundred U.S. dollars.)

On the flight from Kinshasa, I got speaking to some Asian businessmen who were doing the same trip, and was congratulating myself on good contacts made, to be filed away for future use.

When I arrived at the hotel, a modern building which could be in any city in the world – no atmosphere, no hint of Portuguese culture or history, I checked in and went to my room, showered, and tried to sleep, which proved impossible. There was too much turning over in my head, thinking of the searches made, and wondering as to why they did not search my canary-yellow holdall. I eventually got dressed and went for a walk along the old walls adjacent to the hotel, giving a good view over the river and the main part of town. I had convinced myself that I would be watched to see if I had an accomplice, or to pass whatever they thought I was smuggling, to a third party. I spent a restless afternoon, lounging about the hotel, had a meal early, and turned in, to a fitful sleep.

Next afternoon, on checking in at the TAP desk and going to the departure lounge, I was quietly pleased that the police had let the matter drop. They hadn't! A police sergeant, in all his finery and colourful uniform, appeared at the departure lounge, and asked me to accompany him. I was mortified, as I was speaking to the Indian gents from the first leg of the voyage, and now all hope of having a good contact had gone west. I was taken to the basement of the building, and into a small room. Five big men in civilian clothes came in, and started searching my jacket, told me to take off my shoes, went through every item of my holdall, and then started tapping my shoe heels. They must have thought I was James Bond! That was it! I lost my temper, and started calling them every less than polite name I could think of. They were completely taken aback, glanced at one another, and then quickly stuffed my belongings back into my bag. I was escorted back to the departure hall, just in time to hear the flight being called, and boarded a few minutes later. Goodbye Lisbon, the Salazar mentality had not gone away, next stop Toronto!

When I had checked into the hotel near the airport in Toronto, I opened my case to see if the Portuguese police had gone through it after my check-in at Lisbon. I always carefully packed my bag, putting items in exactly the same place. That way, I could see at a glance if anyone had interfered with it. They had not!

Chapter 18

Canada to Texas

Jack had instructed me to go to the crew quarters at Toronto airport if he was not at the gate to meet me, so I presented myself there, explaining that I was looking for Air Canada chief pilot, and was handed a note. It was from Jack – he was in Switzerland, but would not be back until the next day, and asking me to check into a named hotel, which I did. He arrived the next morning and brought me to the private aircraft area of the airport, where he had his small Cessna. It was on skis, and we took off after a bumpy run over the snow covered runway, into a lovely clear sky. I did not notice the flight much, being engrossed in the whiteness of everything – such a contrast to the heavy green of the jungle I had left forty-eight hours previously. Very shortly we were landing on a frozen lake, in just thirty minutes flight time, after Jack made a circle over his house, pointing it out near the lake's edge, at Orillia, Ontario. The landing was pretty good, landing on virgin snow on the ice, and taxiing to a small canal, where he drove along for about one hundred metres, before coming to a full stop. I was like a child with a new toy, mouth hanging open, enjoying the performance, and Jack enjoying my obvious wonderment. He calmly got out of the plane, grabbed a rope that was on a stake on shore, and casually tied the nose of the Cessna to the rope, just as I used to tether cows at home during my school days, and he beckoned me to follow him up the garden to the back door of his house. His wife opened the door, having been warned that they were having a visitor from Africa for Christmas. Jack deliberately had not told her that I was Irish, and enjoyed the look of surprise on her face, when she exclaimed 'but you are white'!

They both excelled themselves, along with their two daughters, in their hospitality. I had only one small problem! I arrived from temperatures of about 40 centigrade and very humid, to about minus 25 centigrade in a little over forty-eight hours, and had no warm clothes. Jack kindly provided me with a zip-up 'bunny' suit, which I virtually lived in for the next week, except for Christmas day, which I spent dozing in a very comfortable lounger, his Christmas present from his wife, while I worked off my jet lag.

They did Canada proud in their hospitality, showing me around the locality, and introduced me to a friend, an ex-colonel in the British army, who did a little wheeling and dealing in bits and pieces. I showed him some ivory pieces and butterfly paintings which I had brought with me, and he bought the lot. That paid for the trip. He asked me to bring him some more if I ever came back. I supplied him with quite an amount over my next few visits, until his market was reaching saturation point. During my next visits, Jack and a friend took me north of Sudbury in his plane, this time on floats, taking off from the lake, and ninety minutes later landing on a lake by his holiday hide-out. It was a lovely big log cabin with one bedroom and a huge kitchen and dining- room. Scattered around the main house were nine log cabins, complete with pot-bellied stoves, beautifully done up, built of great big varnished logs, with four bunk beds in each cabin. There even was an ice house – a small cabin with a door one had to crawl in through, one metre thick walls packed with sawdust in the middle. In winter, he just left the door open, with a good steel mesh to deter animals, and the store became an ice house. In summer, he closed the door, and it retained the coldness, being so well insulated. The sauna house was beside the lake, so it was simply a question of rolling in the snow, or in summer, jumping into the lake. There were various canoes which I put to good use on subsequent visits. Jack and his friend were worried one evening when I had not returned a hour after dark. I had been out paddling in a canoe, enjoying the peace, watching the beavers make their nests and barriers on the streams into the lake, and finally visited a cabin on the far shore. There, a French Canadian was caretaker for the owner, and he kindly offered me a beer. One led to another, which led to several more, until, long after dark, we heard the shouting on the lake. My two colleagues were out looking for me, their searchlight sweeping the still waters. They were impressed that I had found the only other source of beer on the lake, and gave me a tow back in their motorboat.

I still had a fair bit of ivory and butterfly paintings in a big metal box, and I had a contact in Houston, Texas, so I headed for there. First, I took the opportunity to visit a cousin at St. Catherines, spent a few days with him, and saw the Niagara Falls. After seeing the Victoria Falls, these were a real let-down, about one third the height of Victoria Falls.

I had to take a taxi to the border to cross to the great U.S. of A. There I met a slight hitch. Customs enquired if I had anything to declare – the taxi driver answered for me in the affirmative. On seeing a big box of ivory pieces, they asked a lot of questions. I had the answers ready in the form of invoices for all, with the prices in the Zaire money, also called Zaires. As it was not a negotiable currency, they had no record of it, and spent a long time looking for the exchange rate, finally came back to me asking what the rate was? I gave them one, adjusting somewhat (a lot) in my favour. Some more calculating produced an amount of duty so small that it was not worth the paperwork, and they gave me a free pass.

Next stop was New York City on a Trailways bus, and after a few days there, I had a self drive delivery to my destination, Houston, Texas, where I had been given a contact to sell the ivory. These delivery trips were a cost effective way of travelling, and I had four days before delivering the car to its owner, at no cost to me other than the petrol.

My contact was a manager of a big apartment complex who gave me an empty apartment for a week for free. I left the ivory with her to sell and made my way back to Zaire – never to see her or the ivory again. On my next trip back, about two years later, she had vanished without trace.

Chapter 19

Back to basics '78

I spent a wonderful week with Jack and his family, hogged their hospitality, even his Christmas gift from his wife, a lovely lounger chair, in which I spent most of Christmas day, jetlagged. That day, Jack pestered me to phone my mother, and despite my trying to explain to him that he did not understand the Irish phone system, he persisted. The normal method of phoning on Christmas day in Ireland was to book a call with the local post office, which had restricted opening hours, otherwise one had no chance, as all calls had to go through the post office switchboard. For weeks before Christmas, notices appeared in the national press to book ones call. Finally, to get a little peace and to get back to 'my' comfortable chair, I dialed International and gave the lady the name and number in Ireland. To my surprise, she had the spelling of my little village all correct first time, and said she would call me back in ten minutes. Eight minutes later, she called back, and put me through to our local Irish post office. The postmistress there was surprised to hear from me from Canada, but told me that my mother was at a cousin's house for Christmas, and she would put me through to that house six kilometres away! My surprise was no greater than my mother's when I spoke to her. That made her day, and mine. Thanks, Jack!

Soon afterwards, the Irish phone system was overhauled, leapfrogging to a 'state of the art' system.

I bade Jack goodbye, and travelled to New York to pay a visit to my uncle who was terminally ill in a hospital in New Jersey. I was glad to see the family again. It was my uncle who had sponsored me as an immigrant to the U.S. years previously, and who went to great lengths to make my trip to my chosen new land, as comfortable as possible. I spent a few days with them before continuing my travels to Houston, Texas.

On the return trip, again with the Portuguese airline, TAP, there were no problems at the airport, and I had a connecting flight to Kinshasa within hours. I spent only one night in Kinshasa before getting the flight back to Kisangani. The contrast between the cold in North America, and the heat there, even compared to Kinshasa, is difficult to describe. As the plane door opened, it was again like a boxer hitting one full-on in the face, and took a few minutes of adjusting, mentally and physically.

About this time I met a few Canadians who were flying helicopters from Kisangani, setting up radio beacons along the equator line, bringing radio reception to the masses – a very laudable task. Their inexperience was their downfall, as they had not thought through the local problems. Apparently, some brain in Ottawa had decided that this would be a good way to spend Canadian aid money. These beacons were on tall masts at intervals along the equator line, powered by diesel motors that ran for three weeks without refueling. That was all the time they ran for, as there was no way of getting diesel to the masts through dense jungle without a helicopter. They had not thought of the problems of supply, and forty million dollars were wasted. This is indicative of many aid projects in Africa, where people in offices in the western world draw up plans, only to have their projects totally wasted due to lack of local knowledge.

Within a week, it was back to business, planning another trip, hoping to get good ivories, and making a nice profit. My local man assured me that there could be quite a lot of ivories to be had not too far off the beaten track on the road to Bunia, a town near the border of Uganda, not far from Southern Sudan. We were to go as far as the junction of the road going north to Isiro, a distance of some three hundred kilometres. There was only one slight problem – the army was searching for rebels, a frequent occurrence in the north, as there, the locals had never taken to the Mabutu regime. We were to travel at night, wherever possible, something I would never consider under normal circumstances, but in Zaire, who was to say what was normal? The dangers of ending up in a hole, or river, meeting unfriendly animals or natives, was far greater than during daylight hours. However, circumstances obliged, so off we went, early one evening. I soon regretted my decision, as the road was in an awful state, even by Zaire standards, and the going was tough. It being the middle of the rainy season, there were no vehicles on the road, and it was almost impassable.

It was only about six hundred and fifty kilometres to Bunia, in the mountains, where tea, coffee and every vegetable imaginable grew in the cooler climate, but they could not get them to market in Kisangani. The few trucks that did get through, after up to three weeks on the road, often found their vegetables ruined by the time they got to market.

We struggled on most of the night, and at dawn, drove to a small space off the road, where we would not be seen by passersby, and settled down to sleep as best we could, exhausted, despite the rain coming down so hard it bounced a metre off the ground. The incessant thunder of the rain on the cab roof was like a lullaby to me, and I slept the sleep of the dead for most of the day. After a meal of bread, a tin of pilchards and a little water, we were on our way again – more mud, slithering and sliding, crossing bridges, some of which consisted of only two parallel logs to drive over. There, I had my man out front, guiding me under the headlights, easing me over – a centimetre this way, a centimetre that, until we reached the other side. The adrenalin was pumping hard, as a slip of the wheel on the wet tree trunk meant disaster. Twice, we had to walk back several kilometres to retrieve planks from the bridge just crossed, to put in the big gaps on the bridge we had arrived at. There was no question of turning the Land Rover about, as we were in dense jungle, with only a narrow track, without space to turn. We had a big problem on one bridge, where we were lifting the planks as we progressed over the bridge, to lay in front, but came to a great hole which seemed insurmountable.

There was a large gap, which I was convinced we could not cross. There we were, stuck more than half way across, and no way of going back. It was a low point, morale wise. I was out front, trying to retrieve a plank, when the African jumped into the cab, revved the engine, and the jeep roared forward. I had no option, and automatically threw myself sideways to avoid being hit by the bull bars. There was only one place to land – in the river. It was fast flowing, and in a second, I found myself being swept away. Luckily, I was washed against a log, and was able to pull myself out, with no more damage done. I slowly made my way back along the river bank to the bridge, hoping that there were no crocodiles sleeping on the bank, while not daring to venture into the jungle, as one could lose all sense of direction in the dark, never to come out alive. By the time I got back to the bridge, my Irish temper had worked up a good head of steam, which I fully vented on the poor unfortunate waiting for me. When I cooled down a little, I had to agree with his irrefutable logic. The Land Rover was across the bridge – how it jumped the gap, I'll never know, but there it was! The rain had eased off, so we continued on in daylight, hoping that we were out of the 'security' zone. By mid afternoon, we had reached the area where we hoped to find ivory riches.

Two fruitless days later, we decided to call a halt, as there was no sign of ivory, nor were the locals in any way enthusiastic about any forthcoming. There was nothing for it but to retrace our steps, empty handed. The trip back was not the most inviting ever – going over all that effort again, and if we were lucky, arriving back in Kisangani in a few days, empty handed. Fate was not to be so kind! We crossed several rivers without mishap. Travelling during daylight was a lot easier, but not easy. On the second day of our way back, we came to a fairly big river which had a few planks over two great big logs, which we had crossed several nights previously without mishap. This time was another story. Half way across, one of the logs suddenly gave way, crashing into the waters below. The Land Rover was right alongside it, with me hoping it would not land on its roof, crushing me. As luck had it, it landed on my side, with water immediately threatening to drown me, giving me great incentive to climb out the other open window as fast as I could. The river was only about three metres deep, leaving the possibility to recover the Land Rover without too much effort. I quickly made for the river bank, where we both sat for a long time discussing our options.

We finally decided that it could be hauled out, if we could recover the Tirfor and cable. It was the African's turn to enter the river – I had had a bellyful of rivers by now, and besides, if there were crocodiles in the vicinity, I would soon find out! He had no choice but to venture in, doing a great job of diving to recover almost all our equipment, hauling it all to the far bank, near a village some one hundred and fifty metres further along. We were able to set up our tent for the night, just a little the worst for wear.

The next morning the work began in earnest. We secured the Tirfor cable to a tree, and slowly righted the Land Rover, and hauled it to the river bank. Once righted, with very little damage, it made our job a lot easier. It took another full day to haul it from the river, securing it on the bank. The next two days were spent in stripping the engine and diesel tank as far as we could, to get the water from the system. During all this time, the Africans of the village had great amusement watching us, and were in awe of the power of the Tirfor, but never even offered to help in any way.

We finally had it all re-assembled, and holding our breath, hoped for the best, and turned the motor. Amazingly, it fired up after a few false puffs, and after running the motor for a while to make sure the tank was clear of water, we were on our way. No sooner had we began to move away than some villagers waved us down in the traditional fashion, wanting a lift. My gestures to them were less than diplomatic, nor did I stop to give them a lift. Some communities refuse to help themselves, and certainly not others, but eventually it rebounds on them. Many hours later we were back where we had started, with ourselves and the Land Rover the worse for wear, a lot wiser, and poorer.

Chapter 20

Kolwezi 2

I had spent the previous year since the first invasion of the Katanganese to Kolwezi in trying to get back a little of what I had 'donated' to the rebels in May '77, I was slowly getting on my feet again. I had reimbursed Tony for his loan from proceeds of a trip to Kisangani area. I was back in the Katanga/Kasai area, had another good truck, and had made a successful trip to Kinda, some way beyond Bukama, where there was a lot of swampland. The crocodiles there were not the biggest, but they were plentiful, and the locals there had kept the skins properly – well salted and damp, so as not to dry out. If the skins were dry, they were liable to crack, and impossible to work with in Europe.

There was some ivory as well, not big tusks, about six or seven kilos each, but presentable. Much bigger tusks were on the elephants from the savannah further north in the region of Nyunzu, west of Kalemie.

Heading towards Kolwesi, I remembered vividly the previous year, where I had become a victim of the Katanganese at the airport there. At the Impala hotel, I had a good meal, a nice room, and the truck was secure for the night. Next morning I joined a person I knew from Lubumbashi

KOLWEZI 2

for breakfast. He was dealing in compressors for Atlas Copco, trading with the mines. With only four hours drive to Lubumbashi, and relative safety for the consignment, I was in right good form heading out. The airport is five kilometres east of town, where I had been bushwhacked one year and one week previously. Incredibly, there was a roadblock at the exact same location as the previous year. On stopping, it did not take long to have my worst fears verified – the Katanganese rebels were back again. This time they were more disciplined and better armed. Obviously they had made good use of the seventy trucks full of cobalt that they had liberated the previous year on their way back to Angola. They had sold it on the world markets when the prices shot up due to the world shortage created by them, and equipped themselves well. Some were dressed in Zaire army uniforms, helping with the confusion.

Happy days! Who says lightning never strikes twice? Here I was again, walking back to Kolwesi with all I was allowed to take – my boots, socks, pants, underwear, T-shirt, and my passport, a good walk in the heat, but then I had no option. A small twin engine plane was coming in to land. I recognised the plane as being one based in Lubumbashi. As it was near touchdown, almost at stalling speed, some idiot of a rebel soldier shot at it. Pierre had the presence of mind to give the engines full throttle and keep on going for Lubumbashi, just a short hop away. I heard later that was the first indication anyone had of the second invasion. Sounds like a religious revivalist session, but believe me, it was not funny. Finally back at the Impala Hotel, being greeted by my breakfast companion, I broke the news to the horrified Europeans. It was just one year and one week, at the end of the rainy season, and I suppose intelligence should have told them that it was on the cards – but then, sometimes intelligence can be very stupid. I learned later that the rebels had been in the area for weeks, grouping, staying in their surrounding villages, while no one in authority was any the wiser. Someone took their eyes off the ball! (The Zaire army commander was later shot for incompetence)

The next week was not the most pleasant ever. The rebels swarmed all over the place, demanding passports, money, watches, and above all, radios. Any engineer or person in any position of authority, was taken away. They left little old me alone, a tourist who spoke no French, no Tschiluba, and no Swahili, and at which I was at pains to let them know. Things were going from bad to worse at the hotel, with some of the staff having disappeared, more being shot, and food becoming a problem. We were confined to the hotel, pure boredom, speculating on what was going on, with rumours flying higher than Sputniks. Every day there were more bodies laying about the rooms, and the smell and the flies made for a less than pleasant environment. Shooting could be heard all day, and we could only guess about what was happening. Some of the Europeans disappeared, whether by their own efforts or been taken away by the Katanganese in the hotel, I do not know. Finally we were given some leeway as the pressure was put on, with the Zaire army on the ground, and broadcasts from our one hidden radio saying that foreign troops were on the way. On day seven, planes could be heard, French Foreign Legion paratroopers dropped into the centre of town, too late to save the first of a group of thirty-five men who were lined up to be shot. The French Foreign Legion had travelled almost non-stop from their base in Calvi, Corsica. There was some resistance around the hotel, but the Legion quickly and very professionally, secured it. Chaos prevailed in the town after that, with Moroccan, French, Senegalese, Togolese and Chadian troops all over the place within a few days, having taken the airport without much trouble. They put a machine gun post on the roof of the hotel, where I had taken to sleeping, hoping that it would be safer there than on the ground floor, if any fighting occurred in the hotel. I was rudely awakened at dawn on the second day of the French Foreign Legion arriving. The machine gun was working overtime, with the Zaire army soldier manning it totally excited, ejecting empty shells at a tremendous pace, and blowing hell out of an armoured personnel carrier a little over two hundred metres away. The FFl officer in charge could not get him to stop, until a kick in the head to the gunner had the desired effect. It turned out that the personnel carrier had about twenty soldiers all over it. They were Zaire army, but in the half light, the gunner did not bother to have it verified, and had the time of his life - for three minutes. A day or two later, Belgian paratroopers landed at the airport, making a secure zone in that area, where they began evacuation of several thousand Europeans.

  The rebels were all but beaten out of the town, some at full speed, and others giving as good as they got, and until things quietened down a bit, chaos reigned! Bodies were everywhere, many stinking in the hot sun, having been there for up to a week or more, feeding the dogs, rats and vultures. At the new European quarter, I was assisting in checking out houses, looking for anyone who might still be alive. One house opposite the army barrack was crammed with bodies – men, women, Europeans and Zairians, at all sorts of angles, limbs jutting out as they were mowed down by machine gun fire from outside, slaughtered without as much as a thought. The stench was awful. Trying to get the bodies out, stiff and tangled and smelling to high heaven is something I hope never to have to do again. One woman, a Frenchwoman, I think, who was at the bottom of the pile, was, miraculously, still alive. Unfortunately, she had lost her mind and had to be taken to a hospital. I'm sure she never recovered!

A few days later, I was among a truck full of people on my way to Lubumbashi, wondering what next!

Chapter 21

Evacuation?

I finally arrived in Kinshasa after more than a week of hairy living in Kolwesi, when the multi-national force arrived to save the situation from the second incursion just a year after the first invasion by the Katanganese. The flight in the Argusy, apart from a few anxious moments in Kananga where we wondered if we would be refuelled or not, was smooth.

On arriving at Kinshasa airport, there was chaos! Many airlines flying anywhere near Zaire had planes there for the evacuation, and any that overflew en route from South Africa to Europe, had at least one 747 or DC10 on the runway, taking out many thousands of Europeans. Most were Belgians, with a good mixture of Greeks, Italians, some French and a smattering of all sorts. I had never seen so many planes stacked together. Also taking up more than a little space on the single runway were three C5's, about ten C141's, - massive transporters of the United States Air Force, and a collection of small private jets and prop planes. The huge American cargos were carrying 'band aids' for Kamina Base, in north Shaba. Both Kinshasa and Kamina Base runways were constructed to U.S specs to allow for the possible landings of moon rockets, in the early days of space travel, in the

EVACUATION?

event they had to do emergency landings. Three and a half kilometres was long enough to carry a lot of aircraft, and they could take off back-to-back if necessary! The Zairian Air Traffic Control had never had so much work to do, and inevitably, got things in a right mess very quickly.

I was asked to accompany a pilot to assist in the Otrag small turbo-prop, and was trying to get clearance to taxi for fuel, while in front of us was the American Ambassador in a Beechcraft twin-engine who was trying to get clearance for take-off, destination Kolwesi. He was told he would have to wait, while we were given orders to move on to the runway for take-off. The pilot protested that we needed fuel, while the Ambassador was told to taxi for fuel. What followed was the most undiplomatic language I ever heard from an open radio. The U.S. Air Force was immediately instructed to take over the control tower, by force if necessary. There was radio silence for ten minutes and then a cool professional air controller's voice of the U.S. Air Force took over. The confusion was quickly sorted, with the Ambassador getting priority take-off clearance, while we moved to the refuelling bay.

When that was done, I made a bee-line to the Intercontinental Hotel. There were a good crowd in the lobby, a lot of to-ing and fro-ing, with many people with the lost expression of refugees.

I was pleased to see some friends, mainly pilots, at the bar, and wangled myself a beer from one of them. It is not easy to join a company at a bar with not a red cent to one's name! All the talk was of the evacuation and how many planes were at the airport.

I was not long at the bar in the hotel when a well spoken Englishman approached me, enquiring about how he could get out of the country. As I had an evacuation number and was waiting for my call sometime that evening, I told him 'sorry, can't help' but directed him to a French pilot. He was not much the wiser when he came back to me thirty minutes later, and invited me to join him for a meal. I gladly accepted, as for the second time in a little over a year, I was totally, stoney, broke. The Katanganese had left me in exactly the same state as the previous year, with boots, socks, jeans, underpants, T shirt and passport. A meal offered meant that there was a God, and hope shone – from small acorns, etc!

And so it happened! Leo was there to set up a diamond buying company, but his timing was not the best. During the meal, he gave me a general outline of his project, stating that he wanted to continue with it, and asking me if I was interested in acting as his man-on-the-ground there. I found out later that he had spent the thirty minutes at the bar, before coming back to me, asking the others, mainly Otrag employees, their opinion of me. Seems I got a reasonably good report! I quickly told him that I was interested, but sorry; I was broke, no funds, and waiting for my number to be called. He offered to pay my hotel and expenses while we worked out a strategy for setting up the organisation for buying the precious stones. I mulled over the offer for all of seven seconds, before letting my generous nature get the better of me, and accepting. It was a huge advance of thirty minutes previously. Here I was, a flat broke evacuee, being offered a good job, wages, and a chance to make a lot of money, with a fair bit of excitement sure to be thrown in for good measure. Luckily I have a great guardian angel, who must have been working overtime again that day.

The next morning, after a good sleep in a comfortable bed, knowing Leo was paying for it, had me in the best of humour. That came to an abrupt halt by a hand on my shoulder, and Klaus literally dragging me to the door.

Chapter 22

Evacuating US after Kolwesi 2

I was just strolling into the hotel foyer after a leisurely breakfast, when my shoulder was roughly grabbed, and there was Klaus, propelling me towards the door. He insisted in my going with him to the American Protestant Mission in Gombe, a high mountain suburb of Kinshasa. There they had radio contact with the workers on the Inga-Shaba power line, who had almost completed the massive power work. This line went from the falls near Matadi, by the only sea port of Zaire, on the Atlantic coast, about two thousand kilometres to the copper mining region in Shaba. It produced more power than all of Italy, France and Spain combined, and was being constructed by an American company. I had seen some of the crew in the Intercontinental Hotel some months previously. They were real hicks, trying to pick up air stewardesses from various airlines in the hotel lobby – a really sophisticated lot, with their cigarette packs stuck in the arm of their T shirts.

In double quick time, we were at the Mission house, and they had good radio contact, thanks to the high elevation. The power line people were afraid that the Katanganese would attack them at any time, which was with some justification. Something had to be done quickly. I suggested that we could have a DC4 if it was in the area, and we headed for Tony's house, the same man who had helped me financially the previous year. He had two planes, a DC3 and a DC4. Unfortunately, the DC4 was up north, but the DC3 was available.

Tony agreed to the idea, and he and I headed for the airport. The plane was all ready to go, fully refuelled, and with him as the pilot, we were quickly airborne. Once a good altitude was reached, he had good reception from the power line camp on the frequency given to us by the Mission. Tony instructed them to bulldoze a runway within the perimeter of the camp, as there was no other place to land nearby, and it was too dangerous to try to head for a landing spot some distance away. The 82nd Airborne was on its way in the shape of the Fighting Irish! Three hours later, we were nearing the camp, and radio contact verified that the runway was ready. It was easy to find, despite there being no radar in the area. Nearly all flights in Zaire were on a 'dead reckoning' basis, after leaving the established airports. We just followed the high power line. We made a low pass over the camp, Tony was satisfied that there was enough runway to land, and we came in for the final approach, just missing the perimeter fence, and coming to a bumpy landing, stopping well short of the opposite fence, before doing an about turn ready for take-off.

I had just opened the tail door when the first people to jump in were the same men who were trying to use their non-existing charms on the air stewardesses some time before in Kinshasa. Such gallantry! They were all ready, bags and all, but Tony refused to take any luggage. They had no option but pile in as best they could. There were too many of them, so it was decided that myself and six others would take two jeeps back along the track, as otherwise the plane would never clear the bush. A Cat D8 bulldozer was used to knock down the fence to give more space for take-off, and with the engines at full revs, the plane took off like a lazy bird, slowly rising over the bush, gaining height as it circled above us.

We were now on our own, so having made sure that we had enough water and petrol, with some food, we headed back along the power line. Meantime, Tony had radio contact with Kamina Base, the military air base in north Shaba, as soon as he got height, notifying them that we were leaving. Two hours later, making good speed back along the track by the power line, we heard the helicopters coming looking for us. They landed in a clearing a few kilometres ahead and we all piled aboard, after putting hand grenades in the jeep engines, and taking cover behind trees, making sure the jeeps were useless. At the base, I was bunkered with a Greek who worked as a civilian there. He was a very hospitable man, and he and his native wife with their three children, were a joy to see. They were very happy with their lives together.

Two days later, I had a lift in an Air Force plane to Kinshasa. Then it was back to the Intercontinental Hotel to see if Leo was still there.

Chapter 23

Diamonds

The next few days were relaxingly interesting. Leo and I met many times to discuss the prospects, and to try to round off the rough edges to enable us to get the project up-and-running. He needed a permit from the Government of Zaire to purchase and export the raw material, which, he assured me, was to be provided by someone very close to the big boss – Joseph Desiree Mobutu Sese Seiko, Kuku Nbengu wa Za Banga, then President and ultimate dictator of Zaire. As the plan unfolded, it transpired that the purchases were to be from along the border with Angola, with a base in Tshikapa, just inside the Zaire border.

There is a long narrow strip of land where many excellent quality diamonds were found, just inside the Angolan border, DeBeers run, and there was a lot of smuggling going on. With the Zaire border being a few kilometres away, it was the obvious place to sell the illicit goods. It was also a very dangerous area, with Dr. Savimbe rebels making the occasional raid there to profit themselves and their cause. Sometime later, five British mining experts were killed in such a raid. It was these same diamonds that prolonged the war for thirty years, by allowing 'blood diamonds' to be sold in the international market, with a result of total misery to millions of people. (The international community have since set up a system which helps to arrest the sale of such diamonds). Plans were made to have a buying office in Tshikapa, hopefully, and almost certainly, supplied with a lot of the large gem-quality stones from across the border. Security was my remit, with the safe passage for export to Europe – i.e. Antwerp, the centre of diamond buying and selling in Europe. Sales were to be channelled through his family who had a diamond buying, cutting and polishing business there. Arrangements were made for the safe passage through the airport at Kinshasa. The consignment from Tshikapa was to be flown from the strip there to the airport at Kinshasa, and to taxi directly to the plane ready for departure to Brussels. Some phone calls were made to my friend Jack in Canada, who as chief pilot for Air Canada, and who flew 'bush' north of his home in Orillia, could give me some advice and price indications for a high-wing six seater plane.

Well established rivals in the market were the South African mining giants, DeBeers. They had an office in central Kinshasa. As usual with them, security was tight. Information as to their buying and selling was, literally, worth its weight in diamonds. They underestimated the ingenuity of my Zairian friend, Michel, a Baluba, from Shaba province. He was like a brother to me, in the true sense, who got me, the dumb European, out of many scrapes. He checked out the situation, and found that the personal secretary of the chief in DeBeers office was a very comely lady, and he quickly made friends with her. His natural charm worked wonders. Soon we had the daily/weekly reports of the sales of DeBeers. Leo was very impressed, but no matter how much he wanted to know how I got this very commercially sensitive info, I maintained my silence, saying that was my department, so leave well enough alone. He was obliged to accept this modus operandi.

Leo made a trip to Europe, while I took off to Tshikapa to sound out the lease/purchase of some ex-colonial houses there. These buildings were to be used by a diamond buyer and some other staff, including some security and one or two local staff. The town was only a few kilometres from the Angolan border, in an area controlled by Savimbe, in his bid to oust the Government in Luanda. The airstrip was adequate, if a high wing aircraft was used. The only real concern was the security of the diamonds, but it was agreed to keep the buying period short, just hours before the plane departure, to minimise risk. Dealers would soon get used to the dealing times, and no-one was ever in a rush in Africa. Tomorrow means another day, and nine o'clock means another time, using the well known tendency of Africans to tell one what they thought one wanted to hear. Trying to differentiate between European time and African time did not seem to help much.

Leo and I met in Brussels Sheraton Hotel in Place Rogier to iron out some details. He had been to report to his relatives in Antwerp and now was to meet with his big Zairian contact who was to get him his permit for the diamond business. I was not party to the meeting, but Leo assured me that, even having been put off once again, that the necessary permit would be forthcoming. This was despite several warnings from Michel that Leo employed too many people from Shaba, instead of from M'bandaka, Mobutu's region, where the language was Lingala. Tschiluba and Swahili were not the favourite languages of the President.

(Years earlier, I had been sent from London while working with Cementation Company, making foundation works for the Brussels Sheraton Hotel, and I was pleased that it stood the passage of time well)

Things all came to a head when I got a message from 'someone' in downtown Kinshasa shortly after my return from Brussels. A few hours previously, at dawn, a burnt-out Mercedes Benz was seen on the way in from the airport and the carcass of a body lay alongside. The car had been forced to stop by an army roadblock, and it was known exactly who was in the car. The driver was sent scurrying with the news, after watching his employer being shot and skinned alive, leaving the body beside the car. The red ants did their work well, leaving but a carcass a little later. The victim must have gone through an agonising time before dying, with flesh eating ants crawling all over his skinned body, into his eyes, and every orifice, while he was powerless to help himself. It was quickly verified that he was the nephew of President Mobutu. This was disturbing news, as it showed that Mobutu had lost control of the army, and some unrest could be expected. It was worse for Leo, as it turned out that the corpse was Leo's contact and guarantor for the diamond permits. He was also the only person ever to have bought a Lockheed C-130 Hercules transporter as a private individual, importing good from South Africa about twice weekly. Most C-130's are for military use.

Leo mused on the situation for some time, and then decided that he must cut any losses. It had already cost him and his family one million U.S dollars. In the meantime, he tried to screw me for the expenses incurred while I was employed by him. I felt like sending him to join Mobutu's nephew, rather than let him go back to his nice house and blonde wife in Gerrards Cross, in the stockbroker belt west of London. So ended another 'job of a lifetime' – as quickly as it had started!

(At the time of his nephew's killing, Mobutu had taken to living on a luxurious barge on the Zaire River, a little up-river from Kinshasa, for security reasons. The barge was believed to be part of the corrupt dealings that led to the U.S. company getting the contract for the construction of Inga-Shaba power line.)

Chapter 24

Rocket Base to Lubumbashi

When my wonderful job ended, I was back to square one. There were a few trips to the Rocket Base, and a trip with awkward sized boxes delivered to the plateau by truck. Getting there was no problem; coming back was a little out of the ordinary. I was heading alone from the base, seven hundred metres up on a flat topped mountain in north Shaba, slowly winding my way down the precarious track cleared by the locals months earlier by machete, hoe, and axes, supplied from the funds of the generous German company, in an effort to get their rocket base operational. I finally reached the track by the river in one piece. Much of the descent was on a track only just wide enough for the truck, with hair-raising drops to one side, and the bends so steep and sharp that one had to try to get around as best one could, then reverse a little on to the little clearance made for the purpose, until the truck finally was around the bend. From there it was relatively plain sailing all the way to Lubumbashi, eight hundred kilometres away, and no guess as to how many days it might take, but I was hoping to do it in less than ten days. Time on the trip did not worry me, as I had plenty of diesel, a good ten ton M.B. truck, and not a care in the world.

A Baluba friend in Lubumbashi, a real gentleman, who had a printing works there, had invited me some time previously to visit his father, who was the village chief, if I ever was in that vicinity. My trusted Michelin map was studied, and calculating that it was only about seventy kilometres off my route, was worth a detour, in the interest of good relations, and my curiosity. Towards my second uneventful day, making good time – sometimes up to thirty kilometres per hour on a decent dirt track, I finally arrived to the chief's house. Unlike all the others, it was a brick built three room building, standing on its own at the edge of the village. On introducing myself, explaining that I was a friend of his son, I was given a royal welcome – with a few drops of the local poison to begin, then a feast of food, until I finally collapsed on the carpet of grass and twigs that made a surprisingly soft bed. The chief was an excellent host who spoke quite a few words of French, so we were on par, trying to converse. My Swahili was improving a little, and that helped with the locals.

I remember it was a Sunday, and in the afternoon, while I was sitting under a banana tree, out of the fierce heat of the sun, he came to me with news which had been spreading over the Tam-Tams. Mbuji-Mayi, not too far away, has one of the largest mountains of industrial diamonds in the world, and outside the restricted area, locals had found lots of good quality gems, just under the surface, and were busy making their fortunes by digging alongside the river. They unearthed good gem stones, having to dig no deeper than one to two metres. The army put an abrupt halt to that. The women's division of the Zaire army had come in two helicopters, set up their machine guns, and happily blasted away at the locals of Mbuji-Mayi who were busy digging in the unrestricted zone. There is no record of how many died, but it was estimated on the grapevine to be about four to five hundred people, with as many again escaping by jumping in the river, where they took their chances with the crocodiles. When I mentioned this to an English journalist, John, who wrote for the Economist, and was based in Lusaka, who was trying to get a telex out from Lubumbashi some weeks earlier, he accepted it as truth. For some reason, the only report in the international press was in October, five months later, and promptly denied by Mobutu's regime. The Tam-Tam message was grave. The chief said there was a small problem. The army was swarming all over the area, ensuring that there was no popular revolt, and checking the movements of everyone. Even though we were one hundred and forty kilometres from the disaster, he deemed it unsafe for me to continue my journey until the panic had died down. The news took up a great part of the day, with discussions with the chief, and a general gathering, with all having their say, as is the norm with meetings called under their system. We Europeans have a lot to learn from their democracy. As days rolled on, it was obvious that I would be anchored at the village for some time. Luckily, I was in the best possible place to lie low, under the protection of a well respected chief in the area, so had no misgivings. After a few days, time was heavy on my hands. There is only so much to do in a bush village – nothing, apart from smoking, making sure the women did the work allocated to them, and having the craic, (Irish expression of having a good time). The chief, seeing my restlessness, asked me if I had ever seen a lot of diamonds. I replied that I had seen one or two (having been shown through the Diamond Centre in Antwerp, I had seen some lovely gems). He came back some time later with a five litre red plastic bucket, covered in old leaves, and carefully, making sure there was no-one about, spread the contents of the bucket on his wife's waxi (the colourful dress of many African women, mainly made in Dutch Indonesia). I have never seen such a sight! There were kilograms of diamonds – some industrial, many of good quality stones, which would make a man very rich if he had them in Antwerp. Running my hands through this lot, an Aladdin's cave in Shaba! What a feast! Several hours were passed, speculating as to the value of certain pieces, and of ways to smuggle them to Europe. That kept my mind busy for several days, but in the meantime, the chief had carefully gone back into the bush, and buried his trove. At long last, after almost three weeks in the village, with the drums giving the all-clear, it was deemed safe to proceed, and with much relief, I was on my way, after a big feast by the whole village to bid me farewell. The hospitality, as in many African villages, where the population has almost nothing, they share without restriction whatever they have. I was finally on my way, careful to take the routes away from the towns, making the trip longer, but safer. The chief's son in Lubumbashi had already had all the news of my visit, I never found out how! There were no mobile phones or internet in those days.

By this time, Otrag had given up hope of ever seeing me again, thinking that either I was caught up in the aftermath of Mbuji-Mayi, or ambushed in the bush. They were glad to have their truck back!

Chapter 25

History repeating itself

Little by little, there was less need for the Argusy at the rocket base, and to cover some costs, they contracted to supply some U.N. aid along the border with Angola. That was routine work, loading up to four tons, mainly of maize and rice, for flying to small villages' miles from anywhere. Most had no landing strips, and then it was a case of landing on the dirt road going through the village. A routine check was made by flying low over the village, which brought all the locals out to stare at the big plane overhead. Another pass at a much lower altitude was meant to give a signal that the plane wanted to land, but sometimes that did not have the desired effect of clearing the area of goats, cows, chickens and children. The third pass was usually much more effective, with the wing tips just skimming the bush and rondavelles, sending clouds of dust in the air, and scaring the life out of all, who took to the bush en masse, thinking that their last day on earth had come. That gave us many a belly laugh, making the job that much easier. Preparing for one such trip, the plane was all loaded up ready for take-off at Lubumbashi, when the flight crew member who did the external visual inspection reported a problem. There was a crack in one of the twin tails.

Luckily we had not taken off – the crack was about five centimetres wide. That was the end of that plane – just too many landings on rough terrain! Otrag stripped it of avionics, leaving the shell of the plane where it sat, right on the runway.

Here I was – again, high and dry! With work at the rocket base drying up for me, the only solution was a repeat of the previous year – to borrow funds to begin again. Tony obliged once more, and I headed back to Shaba once again to try to replenish my bank account.

I spent a few days in Lubumbashi, and then with my old African sidekick, headed for Kinda, where I knew I could find a supply of ivory and crocodile skins. We travelled by local 'taxi' this time, giving us a lot more freedom and less scrutiny from security forces. It was uncomfortable, being squashed into the front of a small Toyota, with one leg across the tunnel of the prop-shaft. There were only three in the front, which left me in relative comfort – the back being occupied by five men. Sometime after leaving, I had an uncomfortable feeling of something soft against my leg. Trying to catch a glimpse as casually as I could, I finally realised what the problem was. A huge cane rat was draped across the tunnel, and had shifted a little, rubbing up against my leg. Luckily, it was dead – dinner for the driver when he arrived at his destination.

On arriving at Kinda, trading was a lot easier this time, as I had previously had my ground work done with the sellers, who were happy to produce their ivory and crocodile skins and discuss prices a lot quicker. A few days later I had enough bought, and we got the bus back to Lubumbashi. The goods were carefully stashed in sacks of Pili-Pili, the hot African peppers used universally that help cut any stomach infections. People did not want to disturb the sacks, due to the dust from the peppers which could have one coughing and sneezing and sweating for a week, if inhaled. Furniture, bedding, vegetables, goats trussed up, you name it, followed, until the rear of the bus was full to the roof with all sorts of stuff. From there forward was just a press of people, tightly jammed in, one almost literally, on top of the other. My helper and I joined late, not wishing to be in the centre of such a mob, with the only available space being right at the front of the bus. The only way I could make an entry was through the non-existing half-windscreen beside the driver. I managed to get one leg in, but try as I might; there was no room for the other leg. At least I had a ringside seat, was in the fresh air and a view of all coming towards us.

Mostly there were flies, great big juicy ones that splashed on my face, spewing blood and guts all over me. Some of the on-coming trucks gave my heart a few frights by coming almost head-on, and swerving at the last second, just enough to avoid a collision. Every driver was doing his macho thing, playing chicken, but I wished they would choose times other than when I was bound to be the first casualty in an accident. On the other hand, my plight brought peals and screams of laughter from the villagers as we passed through.

All went well, and after many hours, I alighted at the bus station at Lubumbashi, all cramped and barely able to walk. The goods were taken to a safe house in the 'citi' – the African quarter, for safekeeping and packing, ready for the flight to Europe.

I had arranged with a French airline, UTA, to freight the goods to Paris, and had the skins and ivory in separate bales brought to the airport warehouse, weighed and paid for the freight. I had my Airway Bill, and relaxed. I had my ticket ready for the next day on the same flight as the goods. Before boarding, I took the extra precaution of going to the freight warehouse to check on the goods, and was assured when I saw them on a pallet ready for loading. I treated myself to a small bottle of French wine after take-off, looking to better times ahead.

Arriving in Paris early in the morning meant that I had to wait some hours for the freight to be off-loaded and brought to the warehouse. There seems to have been some confusion when I went to claim my freight and to give instructions for forwarding to Antwerp. I had a genuine Airway Bill, but there was no cargo. A few words were spoken, mainly by me, more searches were made, but the cargo was still missing. The French cargo authorities were very put out, and went to great lengths to find the missing cargo. Eventually, they were able to show me several telex's between themselves and Lubumbashi, and showed me in detail the workings of their system – which I had to admit was pretty good – and we came to the conclusion that the goods were never loaded on the plane at all. They made a report, gave me a copy, and said they could do no more, that I had to take it up with the agents in Lubumbashi, Air Zaire (Air Peut-Etre). Here I was, at Charles DeGaulle airport, having spent all day chasing non-existing cargo. The possibility before me was of having lost all, one more time, with my options closing fast! Where to go from here? I needed a break, so I headed for the Emerald Isle to visit family.

Chapter 26

Return, Ilunga – forced stay

After a few days in Dublin visiting family, I finally was able to connect with Lubumbashi by phone to Ilunga, the little Baluba who wrapped my goods and had them brought to the airport. His replies were not satisfactory to me, being too vague. My sixth sense was flying high! The only solution was to go back there to see exactly what had happened, so there I was again, on the first available flight out of Brussels. That happened to be with Alitalia, the Italian national carrier. At check-in at Brussels airport, I was informed of a ground personnel strike at Rome, my connecting point for Kinshasa, and then by Air Zaire to Lubumbashi. I was advised that I could go to Milan, and get a connecting flight from there to Rome, which I did, only to find the airport almost shut down on arriving. I wasn't too worried, rationalising that Alitalia would pay for my hotel, and I would get an onward flight in the morning. I searched all over the terminal for the Alitalia offices, being sent on wild goose chases, until I finally asked an Aer Lingus employee if she could help. She showed me the correct office, and in I marched, only to be told to get lost. That guy did not reckon on my Irish temper – I let fly with all I could muster, almost breaking his desk in two with the force of my fist, insisting on my rights. He got the message, quickly made out a voucher for my hotel and taxi, before apologising, and wishing me good night. The next morning was a bit of a letdown. Due to the on-going strike in Rome, there were no flights until noon. That did not work in very well with my flight to Kinshasa, which was leaving at twelve thirty, entailing another stop-over. It was now Thursday of Easter week, and the next flight to Kinshasa was on the following Tuesday. Alitalia paid for my weekend in Rome while I saw the sights. All was not over yet! On arriving at Kinshasa, the Lubumbashi flight was overbooked, with the next flight in two days time. Alitalia office at the airport did not want to know, leaving about thirty of us to our own devices. I was one of a group who slept by the pool at the Intercontinental Hotel, as the hotel was fully booked. The next morning we all got together and marched into the Alitalia office downtown, angrily demanding that they pay all our expenses up to departure of our flight to Lubumbashi the next day. They initially refused, completely misinterpreting the mood of their passengers, but on reflection, helped by a few well chosen words, they relented. I finally arrived, as quickly as I could, having spent only seven days on the journey.

On arriving, Ilunga evaded me for a few days. I went to Air Zaire (commonly known as 'Air Peut-Etre', owing to their reputation of maybe fly or maybe not) and reported the loss, giving them a copy of my Airway Bill and the UTA report from Paris, and asking how was it possible that the goods which were in their warehouse, ready to go on the plane, did not arrive. It took them three weeks to come back to me with their report – Ilunga had bribed someone in the warehouse and instead of the goods going on the plane, they went out the back gate. No big surprise in Zaire, where the corruption level was about the world's highest. No amount of searching, messages, or going to his home, could unearth the little bilulu (Swahili for insect). Meantime, I was marking time at the Park Hotel.

Option number two was to go to the police, which I did, and made a complaint. The Parquet chief was reluctant to accept the complaint, saying Ilunga had nothing, so it was useless to make a claim. I said that he had a 200 model Mercedes and I would take that as part payment. He reluctantly took the complaint.

Reaction was swift. The next evening, I had a visit to the Park Hotel, by two police in plain clothes, asking me to accompany them to the police chief. Thinking that there finally might be some result to my complaint, I went along, expecting to have some good news from my onetime friend, Ilunga. The interview did not go quite as I had anticipated. I was accused of 'maybe I had something to do with it'. Despite my protests as to the stupidity of that idea, the chief was not convinced. He asked me if I had any money, and on hearing that I had none, asked me how I could stay in a hotel without cash. I point blank refused his offer of bribery, and he retaliated by arresting me and putting me in a cell. There was no charge, just the big boss using his power for his own ends. Obviously Ilunga, the little Baluba, had greased his palm sufficiently.

The luxury of the cell was nothing to write home about. It comprised of a concrete block, 1.60m x 1.60m at the back of the police station, in the open air, with a fine steel door with a grill at the top for air. There were no beds, blankets, or furniture of any kind, just concrete, on the floor, roof and walls. I did have two local ruffians for company, who helped to keep me from going totally insane. As the space was not wide enough for the three of us to lie down all at the same time, one had to stand, or ball up, while the other two slept in turns. Obviously, there was no question of privacy. Toilets were in the grass outside. Visits were arranged by banging on the steel door until a guard opened up, and allowed one person out at a time. Toilet paper was old newspapers, given as a concession to the European, and then it was back to bed. Meal times, as with many African jails, were non-existent. Inmates normally ate when their families brought them cooked food, mostly in the evenings. I had a slight problem here, as I had no family in Zaire. Luckily, the crew of the plane from the rocket base heard of my dilemma, and came each evening with a decent meal for me. This was eaten outside our 'apartment', giving me the only break of the day – apart from nine o'clock each morning. That was when the big chief had me to his office, enquiring if I had any money. He guessed I would break down fairly easily, and make a deal. He guessed wrong each day, so it was back to the 'apartment'.

Things moved along like this in a boringly monotonous way for almost three weeks. My meals were coming regularly, but the complaints from the crew members who brought them got louder. Apparently I had a small personal hygiene problem, which, bearing in mind the circumstances, was understandable. Three weeks without a wash, even after going to the toilet, in the sweltering heat coming to high summer, was not the most hygienic of situations. It was not so bad for me, after the acclimatisation of the first few days, as I stank as much as my cell colleagues, but visitors from outside were almost retching.

The flight crew were getting anxious, as they would soon be on a trip to Europe, which would take about ten days, mainly due to short hops needed for refuelling, and servicing of the Argusy. They finally made an escape plan, as I was losing weight at a great pace.

With the usual meal delivery, they were to hang around, and take two crates of beer with them, offering some to the guards. All went well, with the guards being the worse for wear long before the second crate was finished. On a pre-arranged signal, I was to demand a 'comfort break', which was duly given by the inebriated guard. It was pitch black, just before dawn, and instead of going back to the 'apartment', I stole away with one of the crew to the waiting transport, heading directly to the airport. The crew had taken my bags from the hotel, with my passport and bits & pieces on the mini-bus. Once in the plane, engines were revved up and as it was now first light, with the sun rising quickly on the horizon, we took off for the plateau of the rocket base without incident.

The control tower at the airport was not yet open, and the Otrag crew had carte blanche to come and go as they wished, so we took off as soon as the engines were warmed up. We landed at the rocket base safety less than two hours later, and I was directed to the shower room – curtained off cubicles with a hose pipe for shower effect. Having washed, shaved, and changed to clean clothes, next step was a slap-up meal. Good wholesome food, prepared by a German chef, was almost too much to hesitate over, so I didn't.

I stayed there for three days recuperating, marvelling at the advancements made at the base since my last visit. The runway was complete, unlike when I first 'dropped in' – literally, with Boeing 707's arriving regularly from Munich with all sort of goodies. It was not diplomatic to ask just what was going on, as there was a certain sensitivity about the place. Orbital rockets for peaceful purposes – just tell that to the big bad world! The mess-cum-diner-cum-general living and social club was a magnificent structure, open on three sides, thatched, just as one sees in luxury holiday resorts in the South Sea Islands, and big enough to house all of the personnel there without feeling any way cramped. Then I was airborne again, for Nairobi. The Argusy refuelled there and took off directly for Addis Ababa, their next refuelling stop before Cairo on their hops to Munich and England, where the plane was to be serviced. I checked into the Intercontinental Hotel, getting a small room, a cabana, by the pool, and settled in to enjoy the coming Christmas.

I had lost eighteen kilograms in three weeks, going from 91kg to 73kg. Now I know the ultimate slimming diet, and was thinking of marketing it to Weight Watchers or other groups, as an infallible method, at very little cost.

Across Freedom Park from the hotel was a Convent school, run by Loreto nuns. The big Bwana there was a cousin of mine, so the next day I sauntered along to see her. She had her typical warm welcome, with an immediate 'you look terrible'. Thanks, Anna!

Some days later, I again crossed Uhuru Park, the city park, to the convent. Anna was in the kitchen, weak from laughter. When she finally composed herself a little to tell me the reason for all the mirth, she explained that the old African cleaner woman was dusting in the office when the telex started up automatically (in-coming message). The poor old dear had never seen it work before, so swore blind that it was magic, and promptly took off, leaving the building, never to come back. Too much voodoo!

One Sunday, I went with Anna in her car north of Nairobi to see a Catholic priest from our area in Ireland who had been there for years. His house was right on the edge of the Rift Valley, with the corrugated iron roofed church alongside. Water was a big problem there, and when the water tank, high on stilts, ran dry, he used the water that he had stored in the bath, which was a dirty brown colour, and then prayed hard for rain. The escarpment was about four hundred metres down to the valley floor, and the track of the railway which ran from Mombasa, at the Kenyan coast, to Kampala, Uganda, could still be seen there. Trains were lowered down the steep escarpment by winch on specially constructed platforms, keeping the carriages on an even keel. It was during the construction of this railway that a base camp was used in the centre of Kenya, which blossomed into the city of Nairobi.

Luck was finally on my side. Aer Lingus, the Irish airline, had a Boeing 747 charter from London to Nairobi each Friday night, arriving Saturday morning. This did not give the crew enough rest time before the flight returned to London that same evening, so they had to stop-over for a full week. I was in clover, with six lovely Irish girls, rotating every week for the six weeks I was there, and I took full advantage of the situation. One day, lounging by the pool and acting the eejit with two gorgeous Dublin girls, we noticed a German nearby who was eying the girls. We set up a small drama for his titivation. Both girls, in mini-bikinis, made a great show of putting sun cream on my back, and anywhere else they thought might arouse the German's interest. That done, the two made a big play of going to my cabana with me, until, after a lot of loud discussion, they agreed to go in, one at a time. We entered, put on the radio, and every few moments, loud screeches of pleasure emitted from the cabana. Ten minutes later, by arrangement, there was loud banging on the door; with the other girl shouting that 'it was now her turn'. The look on the German's face when we finally returned to the pool was hilarious. He must have been wondering just what I had that made the two lovelies so attracted to me. Some people just have no sense of humour,!

Exactly one year later, in an Irish bar in New York City, I recognised the captain of one of those crews. He had been re-directed from Boston owing to bad weather, and the crew chose the pub where I was having a meal. Small world!

Chapter 27

Passport

I had asked the Irish Department of Foreign Affairs for a second passport, to avoid being delayed for many weeks waiting for visas to go to Zaire, but the then Minister refused, stating that 'I might do business with South Africa' – despite the sanctions. I just do not know what planet some of these politicians live on – certainly not in real life! My passport was full of stamps, and had another attached to it by the embassy in London some time previously, which was also almost full.

Rather than go all the way to London just to get a new visa, waiting three weeks, and the risk that the embassy there would see the lack of an exit stamp when I left Zaire in the Argusy before Christmas, I thought that the best move would be to return to Zaire via Zambia, where the chances of detailed scrutiny were much less, mainly due to most of the border guards being illiterate. That, with the time frame and cost involved made it a no-brainer, so I was on a flight to Lusaka, and the first available flight to the Copperbelt. All went well. A flight to Ndola and a bus going north towards the border dropped me off some kilometres from the border post. From there it was back to basics – the old thumb out for a lift, if there were any cars on the road. As it still was early morning, I had a good chance to get a lift somehow. There were very few Europeans with a suitcase thumbing on that road, so the first pickup that came along gave me a lift all the way to Lubumbashi. Here I was back in the Park Hotel two months after my quick getaway just before Christmas, wondering what would happen if the police chief 'invited' me to visit him again. I went to see my printer friend whose father I had visited in the bush earlier during the Mbuji-Mayi massacre. He asked around some locals in the know, and within two days I had the all-clear. The police chief had been transferred to north Shaba to a small village when the Governor of the province heard of a European in jail without any charges being brought. My sympathy almost went out to the poor man, stuck in the bush, with his career in tatters, until I thought of my previous visit, and the 'apartment' he had me in for nearly three weeks, so I soon got over that silliness. I was a free man again, but just had to watch the border controls, making sure they would not be too inquisitive about my passport stamps.

I needed transport, and there was no chance in Shaba – nothing I could call a car or truck, which was not battered to hell and back, so the only option was a trip back to Zambia. There were plenty in the Copperbelt which were reasonably well maintained by the mines, so that was the best choice. A Japanese company had offices in Lubumbashi for their mining operation near the Zambian border. I went along to their offices, standing in front of an officious man behind a desk, just like a little schoolboy, until he consented to look up and abruptly asked me what I wanted. On hearing that I would like a lift to the border, he curtly told me that they did not give lifts. That put me in my box! Two days later, I was on the road again that I had travelled two weeks previously on my way from Zambia. I had no trouble getting two lifts which left me at the border. The same Border customs man greeted me as on my earlier visit, and he waved me by, having remembered me. There were several cars which stopped then, finally arriving at Kitwe in the early evening and checked into the Edinburgh Hotel.

It took three days to have a decent Toyota pick-up chosen from the mine office, paid for, and I was on my way back to Lubumbashi. The border crossing was a little bit trickier this time. The man in charge could read, and was not happy with my passport, and turned me back. The trusted Michelin map showed a track which would by-pass any border posts, but coming around a bend, having made a detour of several hours, and thinking that by then I must be well into Zaire, I came up short on a Border post. Nothing for it but face the music! After many questions and much scrutiny of my visas, they concluded that they could let me pass, but first I had to go with one of them to a customs post where they had a stamp to put on my passport. There was no argument, I had no choice. On coming out of the hut, my jaw dropped. My pick-up was loaded high with everything possible to put on it, including goats, bedding, chickens, bags of vegetables and anything else they could pack on, decorated on top by three fat women – without even a by-your leave! I tried to argue with them, making gestures that they get down from on top of it all immediately, but it was soon clear that the three old ladies had no intention of moving. With the customs man in the cab beside me, we headed off along the badly rutted track. I went extra carefully, as I had visions of my new pick-up having broken springs before I had ever had a chance to use it. Finally, in pitch darkness, we arrived at the post. There was no problem in getting my passport stamped again, and in the meantime the kitchen-sink lot offloaded their belongings, and disappeared into the night without even saying 'happy Christmas'. Then it was back again to drop off the Customs agent at his original post, forty kilometres back along the track, after having to pay him for his extra time. I did not mind that – it was worth not being sent back all the way to Zambia. Dawn saw a very tired me arriving at Lubumbashi.

Chapter 28

Lake Mweru June '79

George, a Greek with whom I became friendly, and I were all loaded up for our long stay at Lake Mweru, where he had a house with one of his African wives. We travelled with both vehicles – he in his reliable old Peugeot 404, and me with my trusty Land Cruiser, which I had bought in Zambia. The road was reasonable, it being well into the dry season, and we made good time. He had told me that during the Belgian occupation, it was possible to travel the same road at one hundred kilometres per hour, but not anymore! We arrived at his house, a mud and wattle structure a little apart from the village by the southern tip of the lake, and his wife showed me my room. It was clean, with a hand-made wooden bed, and an old mattress. It was adequate, and beat sleeping in the bush, with the possibility of snakes coming to my tent. After a meal of chicken, we turned in early.

Next morning, all the equipment was off-loaded, stored, and we headed for the lake. His boat was as he had left it. Apparently, the villagers respected their own, as his wife was from there, and it would be safe from harm while she was there. They also appreciated George's work there, keeping the crocodile numbers down, as they had taken several village women and children from the bank of the lake, as well as a few cows. The crocodile's favourite trick was to lunge on an unsuspecting person or animal, drag them down to the bottom of the lake, drowning them, before making a meal of them. We fitted the little outboard, and set out for a trial run. All was fine, with George showing me the more likely places to get the crocodiles. The lake was full of them, and as the waters receded during the dry season, they were more condensed in the diminishing waters. The rest of the day was spent in rigging the beam light by the stern, making sure we could switch it on and off as needed, and getting our gear for the boat ready. This consisted mostly of George's shotgun, and some lassoes for the crocodiles as we shot them, before they sank to the bottom of the lake. We then went for a good meal and siesta, before beginning our night's work.

It was well after dark when we next ventured out, shotgun and cartridges, mostly 1 X, with a few 2 X, sufficient to kill the crocodiles. With the light of our torch, we quickly had all ready, and shoved off. The small outboard pushed us along at slow revs, we moved out a few hundred meters and George switched on the light at the stern, playing it slowly over the water. It did not take long for him to pick out the red eyes of an approaching crocodile. They are like rabbits, attracted to light, and it was easy to pick them out. He calmly allowed the crocodile to approach to within two metres before blasting it between the two eyes. There was a thrash of the tail, before it lay still. George put down the gun, and quickly lassoed its snout, securing it to the boat, before putting the motor in gear and heading for the bank. No sooner had we touched land than he jumped out, and shouting to me to help, we finally got the big monster tied to a tree trunk, where it lay without a move. The operation was repeated, with some input from me, getting used to the routine as the hours went by, until we had twelve crocodiles lined up. It was now about two o'clock at night, so we headed for bed.

First light saw us again at the lakeshore, along with a native helper. Then the real work began – skinning the soft underbelly of the crocodiles. We had very sharp knives, but even so, it took a special knack to dig it in and begin cutting along the side of the stomach, taking care to cut the soft underbelly skin as wide as we could, for its full length. The smell and the white blubber and blood was off-putting at first until one got used to it. The soft underbelly was the part of the skin that the dealers in Europe wanted to transform to bags, shoes, belts etc. in the expensive shops across the world. The remainder of the crocodiles were superfluous to our requirements. The villagers took them, taking any parts they found useful, salting some of the meat for their food, which tasted a bit like a mixture of fish and chicken, and dumping the left-overs in the lake. There the live crocodiles had a field day, gorging themselves on the flesh of their brothers.

Even though George showed me how to skin the crocodile properly, it took me two hours to skin my first one, while he and the African were able to do one each per thirty minutes. By the end of a week, I had improved a lot, but could never be as quick as either of them. The routine set in, with a siesta in mid-afternoon, during the heat of the day, then a meal, and ready for the night's 'fishing' We rarely had to use more than one cartridge on a crocodile, and each night had a good catch of about twelve, enough to keep us busy during the morning, skinning. They were all a good size, between three to three and a half metres long, giving us underbellies up to forty-five centimetres across. It was tiring work, even though I had become accustomed to doing my bit, and enjoyed plugging them between the eyes at a very close range. The smell and blood everywhere took a few days to get used to, but human nature can be very adaptable, and I soon was like a native to the work. The thought of the rewards in Paris was a good incentive.

All went as planned, until one morning when George began to skin a big fellow, it was not dead. It flipped, and caught his arm as he attempted to get clear. Luckily, it was barely alive. I was beside him, turned and saw George with the crocodile trying to bite his arm off. I had got into the habit of carrying a small silver plated .38 that I had been given by an American CIA agent in Lubumbashi, and quickly put a round in between the crocodile's eyes, in the same spot he had been hit the previous night. That did the trick – the crocodile opened his jaw enough for George to free his arm. Luckily, the beast had very little strength left, but there still were considerable gashes along George's arm. These needed immediate attention, and with the help of the village medicine man, some leaves and herbs were applied after cleaning it with warm water and alcohol, and he was strapped up with spider web and banana leaves. He was in considerable pain, but with the help of some locally brewed alcohol, was soon asleep.

It was obvious that George had to take some time to recuperate. We had been over a month at this dirty, stinking work, and I was fed up with it, looking every day at the pile of skins getting bigger, and wondering when we would have enough. The skins were being kept by George's house, under guard. His wife made sure they were well damped down each day, to avoid them drying out and cracking, by dampening the covering burlap bags twice daily. It was time for a pause for all of us. We needed filters and plugs for the engine, as well as fuel and a change of food, so I suggested I go to Zambia, where I could find all we needed on the Copperbelt, as well as give me a much needed break.

(The Americans had listening posts in Ethiopia, presumably listening-in to various countries in the Middle East. Rather than sending their crews on rest and recreation to somewhere like Rome, where there were regular flights, it was deemed more prudent for them to be sent to a quiet spot, where the dangers of loose talk were very limited. There were regular rotations of operatives, most who did not mix in any way with others in the Karavia Hotel, Lubumbashi, keeping strictly to themselves. One operative did speak to me one day, and without asking any questions as to his reasons for being there, told me there were 'on vacation' from Ethiopia. We became a little friendly, and one day he brought me to the U.S. Consulate. There he showed me the gun room, which had a terrific stock of all the best weaponry available. On leaving, he gave me a silver-plated .38 with a stock of bullets.)

Crossing the river Luapula on the small ferry was an adventure. Mine was the only vehicle on it – and I soon found out why! On the Zambian side it was almost impossible to get up the riverbank, but finally made it after a lot of coaxing of the powerful three litre motor, revving it to full speed to get enough momentum to get over the barrier. Then I was on my way, with only two days drive to the Zambian Copperbelt, with much needed rest and recreation. The Zambian Customs had other ideas! Just as I had finished congratulating myself on having beaten the 'system', on a road with no controls, I rounded a slight bent, only to come on a customs barrier – a 'stop' sigh, a tree branch across the road on two sticks with another 'stop' sign, and a little hut. As I stopped, a Customs officer, in a pure white uniform, came out and started questioning me as to where I was going? When told that I was on my way to the Copperbelt, he asked to see whatever I had. A few items of clothes were all I had to produce, along with a screwdriver, pliers and a shifting spanner, which did not satisfy him, so he insisted that I open the bonnet, and take off the air filter, to get at my stash of cash which he was convinced I had hidden there. He was out of luck! The same result went for the heavy rubber mats on the floor-bed of the pickup. Looking under the seats in the cab revealed nothing but pliers, and a screwdriver plus a very greasy rag. I handed it to him, but he did not want to get his uniform dirty. He then took my passport and beckoned me into the hut, lecturing me on the journey, how I had a lot of confidence making that journey without money. I assured him that I had money in Barclays bank in Ndola, and had enough fuel to get there. He went into the back room, leaving me wondering if he had a radio there. It was thirty minutes of anxiety for me, until he reappeared and handed me my passport – presumably having gone through all the stamps and wondering what to do. He told me in a resigned manner that I could go. I jumped into the cab, started up and was just on the point of going forward when he had a brainwave; I had entered! Half of the front wheel of the Toyota was past the stop sign. I had had enough! I was about to run him over, barrier and all, until I saw that he was just going to give me a tongue wagging, which he proceeded to do for fifteen minutes, while I sat there with a soulful face, and made the right noises at appropriate times. Honour satisfied, he then lifted the barrier and I was on my way. Had he accepted the greasy rag I was handing him, he would have found what he was looking for, a 'gift'. Another good day for private enterprise!

Chapter 29

Paris, skins and leaving Jan/Feb 80

I had no problem in Ndola getting all the supplies I needed, it being well served with shops and stores that might be needed for a bush trip. Salt was a big order, with half a ton taking up a lot of the space at the back, along with two forty-five gallon drums of petrol. A supply of canned food was the next best thing, and lastly some more cartridges for the shotgun. After a few days, it was goodbye to the Ambassador Hotel, and I was on my way back to Shaba. There was no point in trying to take the short route going directly north to the crossing just south of Lac Mweru, as I felt sure that the jeep, with its load, could not navigate the steep banks of the river by the crossing.

There was nothing for it but to take the main road to Lubumbashi and then on again to Lac Mweru. I had no problems at the border crossing, as one of the customs officers recognised me from previous crossings, and waved me through quickly on receiving a pack of twenty cigarettes. Not many kilometres from the border post, I could see a car pulled over to the side of the road, with a driver standing alongside, obviously waiting for a lift. As one does in Africa, I slowed down to offer assistance, and was surprised to see a Japanese man. His almost new car had broken down. I got out to have a look, and was about to offer a tow, when I recognised the same man who has been so curt and rude to me some time earlier when I had gone to his office asking for a lift, telling me that he did not give lifts. I smiled to myself, thinking about my revenge. Slowly, I got back in the cab, started my engine and pulled away, with the Japanese man running after me. I allowed him to catch up before shouting to him that 'I do not give lifts' – exactly as he had told me, and hurried on my way. My only regret was that it was not close to nightfall, when he almost surely would have to spend the night by the roadside.

A one night stop in Lubumbashi, and by mid afternoon the next day, I was back at George's house, offloading the supplies. George's arm was much improved, and apart from some scarring, was almost completely healed. He put it down to the use of cobwebs and natural herbs his wife put on it. The next day it was back to the usual routine of shooting about twelve crocodiles per night, skinning and salting them in the morning, until we had several tons ready. I went to Lubumbashi, contacted George's cousin who had a truck and we went back together for the skins. It was arranged that the cousin and myself would go to Europe with the skins, as George, who was born in Zaire, had no passport, and had never left the country. It was up to me on getting to Paris to arrange for the sale of the skins, as I had the contacts. Yanni, the cousin, had no idea of Paris or how to go about selling them. He arranged the shipping, and all went well, with the skins arriving in Paris, and I contacted a buyer.

We met in his office at La Defense and discussed prices. It was arranged that the buyer would take the skins to his factory about one hour south of Paris, and we would go there in two days time when they were weighed, measured, and quality assessed. Meantime, the dealer lent us the use of a very spacious penthouse apartment near the Eiffel Tower, took us to dinner in a very expensive restaurant, and generally treated us very well. Two days later, he drove us to the factory, where we saw the skins being offloaded, counted and measured. We were then taken to a restaurant which did not even have a name, alongside a small river, where I had the best meal ever. The next day was payday, and what a payday! Yanni, reverting to his natural instincts, then tried to have all the money paid to him, but the dealer was scrupulous in his dealings, coming to me to check our deal, before paying out separate checks. Yanni was not at all pleased, nor was I, having worked long and hard for my half share. We parted company in Paris there and then.

Later, having spent a week enjoying myself in Paris, I arrived back in Lubumbashi, and went to see George, curious to know if he had received his money from his cousin. He assured me he had. By this time I was getting tired of Zaire, where one had to try to protect ones back from every angle, never knowing when one could be left on the dung heap, so I decided to quit, via Zambia. I told George of this, and surprisingly, he agreed to drive me to the border. I accepted, and gave him my silver plated .38 as a parting gift. We were on the road early, with my suitcase in the back, heading for the border. Most unusually, there were several customs controls on the route, something I had never seen before. All my belongings were searched at every control, and we were on the road again. After the fourth control, the penny dropped. George had never been checked once. He had volunteered to drive me, and apparently Yanni had alerted the customs that I was to be smuggling diamonds, hoping that I would spend years in jail as a retaliation for 'losing' half the crocodile skin pay-out in Paris. Certain nations have a reputation for being less than 100 per cent honest! Luckily, the customs did not find the hidden space in my suitcase, so I had the last laugh, hollow as it was! I thanked George politely at the border post, wished him well, hoping he would not be searched too much on his return journey, and sent him on his way.

Next stop Lusaka, to think what to do, and consider my future. I was getting tired of Africa at this point, up one day, down the next, getting older, and realising that it was a young man's job. I spent a few days with my old colleague, John, and soon met quite a few people that I knew previously. One of the contacts introduced me to a minor government minister, a very nice gent. He wanted to buy a used Mercedes Benz from South Africa, but could not go there due to sanctions. He asked me if I was interested in buying one for him, I agreed, and we made a deal. I was off to Johannesburg again.

Chapter 30

Car Mess March '80

I had just arrived in Johannesburg from Zambia to buy a Mercedes for a Zambian Government Minister. We had worked out a deal – he would pay in advance in Zambian kwacha, I transferred the kwacha at a good rate over the phone to Leo in Belgium, who trusted me at this stage to do dealings for him. South African Rand would be paid out to me on production of a set of numbers to another 'sleeper' in Johannesburg, I would buy the car, drive it to Lusaka for the Minister, and keep the difference in exchange, and any other extra, for my trouble.

As in many cities, there is an area where almost every second shop is a car dealer. Checking them all out for a day or two had me zoned in on a nice 200D, which was in good condition, and it passed the tests. The deal was done, I insured the car for the trip, and I was on my way – a long boring trip north to Beit Bridge, the crossing point to Rhodesia.

There things livened up a bit, with some security due to the war just ending, and elections having taken place during two days previously. First, I had to go through the formalities of border customs. For a white man, they were just that – formalities. I still had to go in convoy to Masvingo, a rest stop and nothing else on the way. The convoy stayed there, and the remainder of the trip to Salisbury, now called Harare, was done without incident, with a few Selous Scouts as passengers taking advantage of a free ride to the capital, guns sticking out of all windows, just as in the Al Capone films. It was the 10th March, the town was teeming with people due to the elections, and the only place I was able to get a room was at the Feathers Hotel, by the golf course. There were many Africans everywhere, waiting for the outcome of the voting, confident that there would be an African government in power very soon. Their euphoria was understandable, but as later events were to show, sadly misplaced.

After a light meal in the hotel, and a few beers at the bar, and shooting the bull with some locals, it was deemed wise not to venture out that night, so I turned in early. Before I could get to sleep, there was much shouting and crowing going on all over the place. I quickly dressed and made my way to the bar again, where I was told that the crowing was in celebration of Mugabe's win in the elections. Each political party had a sign which could be easily identifiable by any unschooled persons, and Mugabe's party was the sign of the cock. There was a lot of apprehension, some muttering about the kaffirs (derogatory term for Africans) etc., so I took off to bed again. The shouting abated late that night, but I had already decided that I did not want to be in Rhodesia if another war broke out anew.

The only option was to continue on my journey, so at first light I was on my way, heading north for the border crossing with Zambia. The journey was uneventful to Chinhoyi, where I was obliged to wait for the convoy which left about nine o'clock. Since I had not had breakfast, the hotel there was only too willing to give me a good meal. A minor problem was solved when I bartered a bottle of good South African wine for my breakfast, having spent the last of my Rhodesian dollars at the Feathers Hotel.

With a good meal under my belt, I was waiting for the convoy. About 9.30a.m. all were ready to go – myself, and two farmers who lived near Mana Pools, and a couple of light armoured cars. The farmers veered off the main track some distance before Chirundu, to their farms, while I continued amidst shouts of well wishes from the soldiers, their escorting job over. The crossing into Zambia at Chirundu was done in very little time, and I was out of the 'war zone' and in a peaceful country, so now I could relax for the last part of my journey to Lusaka.

All went well for a few kilometres, until soldiers at a Zambian army roadblock directed me through the bush where they had bulldozed a track. They informed me that a bridge had very recently been blown up a little ahead by the Rhodesians, so they had to construct a detour. That meant that my plans for being in Lusaka for that evening were up in the air. A few kilometres along the dirt track, going slowly due to the unevenness of the track, I found out that, literally, my plans were up in the air.

Apparently, the Rhodesians were making one last stand. They must have come back after the Zambian army had cleared the bush track, and set another bomb by the track. My recollection was of me, with the car windows open, head out the window, going up, and up. The laws of gravity finally took over, and the car hit the ground with an almighty crash, landing on its driver's side. My head was more or less where it had been on the way up, still on my shoulders, but descending, it got entangled in the driving mirror. I remember seeing the mirror broken in several bits, then became conscious of my own predicament. There was blood everywhere, and survival instincts dictated that I get out of there as soon as possible. I managed to crawl out the broken windscreen, and stood up, taking stock. I stood there for a good few minutes, thanking God that I was still alive, and then the damage assessment began.

My teeth, all of the top row at the front, were a mess, sticking out at right angles from my gum, in sharp bits. There was no-one around, and the chances of finding a dentist there were slim to none at all, so the reality of the situation was – I had to survive as best I could. There was nothing for it but to pull the remaining stubs out with my fingers, to avoid having sharp teeth sticking out through my lips, which would be even more of a mess! This took a little time to achieve, but was not too bad, as the damaged area was still warm. I donated the bits of teeth to the bush, along with a fair splutter of blood. I was badly shaken, with sore ribs, back, kidneys, and jaw. One side of my face was very painful, but I could see nothing too outrageous in one of the car mirrors.

The next problem was what I should do, where to go, who to see. I thought that the Zambian army might have heard the blast, but the bush is a wonderful sound blanket. Just as I was contemplating spending the night in the back of the wrecked car, a pickup arrived, driven by a Polish farm worker. He kindly offered to take me to the bush hospital, for which I was grateful. On the way, he kept asking questions, while all the time, as much as I could do was to avoid passing out.

Finally we arrived at the bush hospital – a building with two rooms. One was a large ward with beds closely laid out side by side; the other was the deluxe model, with only two beds. One bed was occupied by an African, and I was kindly shown the other. There was no water for washing the blood, no medicals, nothing to relieve the pain. I lay fully clothed on the bed. The sheet was almost black, and I vowed never to get under it. I changed my mind when it started to get dark. The mosquitoes had a field day, gaining free entry through the open hole that served as a window, high up near the roof, being attracted to all that rich Irish blood. It took me over an hour to get my shoes off and get under the sheet, pulled right over my head, to escape the lechers. After some hours, exhausted, I fell into a deep sleep, only waking to broad daylight and a hospital nurse beside me. She explained that there were no facilities, and the sheets were, in fact, washed, but there was no powder to wash them properly. I was able after a while, to give her a phone number of an English friend, John, in Lusaka, in whose house I stayed from time to time. Three days later John showed up in his reliable old Peugeot 404 and took me to his home. I had initially met John in Lubumbashi Post Office when he was trying to send a journalistic report. He wasn't having much luck, and as I was beside him sending my own telex, was able to send his along with mine. We became friends, and had previously stayed with him, at his invitation in his house in Lusaka, Zambia.

John's wife was in England, so he had the run of the place to himself. I had a room, comfortable bed with all mod cons – a massive improvement on the hospital bed. I was unable to lie down due to pains all over, so I spent my time in the armchair. I slept fitfully like this for a week, slumbering most of the day and night, and sipping water occasionally.

There was plenty of time for reflection on the irony of it all – an 'own goal' in a way. I had helped the Smith Government in Rhodesia a few times over the previous few years, and now here I was, in one of their last act of defiance, a victim of their handiwork. On about the twelfth day, hunger pains were getting a bit much, as I had eaten nothing since my breakfast in Rhodesia nearly two weeks previously. John made me some good soup, and after a lot of effort, I was able to eat most of it through a straw. My back, face, ribs were still hurting a lot, but the pain began to ease to such a degree that after another week, I got out and had a short walk. That was a mistake. I crawled back to the house, in a nice suburb of Lusaka, realising that I was more seriously injured than I had previously thought. The only solution was to check into a hospital. Zambian hospitals, for operations or medicines, were out of the question, so I got a Zambian Air flight to Johannesburg, and checked into the General Hospital there, at Hillbrow.

At that time, Hillbrow was a nice area, frequented by nurses and doctors from the hospital, with many good restaurants, and a buzz about the place. Today, it is a no-go area. Several weeks of good attention had me almost back to normal. I was no longer urinating blood, and I could get up and walk a little every day. My broken ribs were also improving rapidly, and the work they did on my jaw bone, with my face all sorts of colours, was beginning to show a little result. All-in, it took three months for me to be on my way, but not before I had settled up my bill, which left me almost on the breadline again.

Chapter 31

Meeting Fred

I was a day patient at the hospital in Hillbrow for some weeks, and met an Afrikaner at my favourite hangout in Santon. He was in a group of people, and noticed my hanging back and observing people, and my Irish accent. He invited me to join the group, ordering me a good stiff whiskey – Irish, of course. Fred turned out to be a very affable man of about forty years, and he invited me to stay as his house-guest nearby. He said he had plenty of space, and that it would be no bother at all, more an asset, as he travelled a lot, and would I mind house-sitting for him while he was out of town? In my position, just finishing with the hospital, it was a gift which I did not hesitate to accept, and arranged to move in two days later. It was not exactly a house, more a great mansion, with a lovely thatched roof, and swimming pool in the back garden. I quickly settled into the guest wing, and to justify my stay a little, got down to the job of cleaning the pool which he had badly neglected. It took several days to get it in pristine condition, but when it was done, Fred arranged a party for the Sunday afternoon. The spit was hauled out from a shed, cleaned down, drinks and food were ordered, and lastly, a heap of charcoal was got for the Braai, - a South African term for barbeque. The Braai was a great success, with a whole sheep on the spit, beautiful women and marvellous weather with terrific dance music setting the tone for the evening. With all the people I met there, nearly all giving me phone numbers to call them, and invitations to dinner, my spirit soon rose from the pit it had been in, giving me a new lease of life. This was living in the style to which I could become accustomed very easily!

I had a diary, not for the usual purpose of jotting down my daily happenings – that would be too dangerous in my chosen line of work if it fell into the wrong hands, but mainly for phone numbers, some addresses and general notes. I found this method more useful than having bits of paper, which could easily be lost. On one of my trips to Zambia some time later, at Kabwe, while waiting for a friend to go to his farm on a money exchange deal, the police took me to their station for questioning. A strange European there was suspicious in their eyes, the Government having used the security excuse for their many shortages of goods. Incompetence would be a better way to describe those shortages. My bag was searched, I was searched, and asked to take off my shirt while they had a good look – presumably to see any bullet damage if I was a mercenary – and then they had a good look in my diary. They asked about the phone numbers given by Fred's friends, and I told them they were phone numbers of girlfriends. They replied that 'no one has that many girlfriends', saying that it must be code I challenged them to phone any of the numbers, asking for the lady by name, but they just let the matter drop, and sent me on my way.

I made my regular visits to the hospital, getting a new set of front teeth fitted to cover the massive space in my gums, and gradually got back to 'normal' – whatever that might be in my style of life. Every few weeks, Fred was off to the Seychelles or somewhere – on 'holiday', leaving me his car. I never did find out what he did, except that he was a director of a big company. I think I found out the company's line of work some time later, when he introduced me to an Englishman, who introduced me in turn to another Afrikaner.

Being well on the road to recovery, I decided to earn a little spare money by doing a few deliveries for Leo in Antwerp. It was very simple. All I had to do was to call Leo every week, making sure that I phoned from a post office or public phone, technologically untraceable at that time, when he would give me a series of numbers and a local phone number, which I would call and arrange a meeting point. When contact was made, each would verify that the series of numbers corresponded, and I was given a holdall to deliver. Another call to Leo got me another series of numbers and phone number, repeating the operation in reverse, where I handed over the holdall to the contact. I was given a reasonable commission per transaction, which Leo wired to me on a regular basis. Each time, there was always over one hundred thousand U.S. dollars or equivalent in the holdalls. It had occurred to me that I could disappear with the holdall, but Leo was a straight individual who treated me well, so I just did the courier work.

Every month or so, I took a trip to Zambia or Zimbabwe, as Rhodesia is now called. There was a steady stream of smallish sums of local currency coming available in Zambia, but things were tightening up there, and I could see problems ahead, especially when 'Belfast', Zambia's chief security officer, who reported directly to President Kenneth Kaunda, 'invited' me to his office for a chat. I thought it best to cease any further operations there for the present. Zimbabwe was another kettle of fish. There things were really tight, with the benefit of experience from the Smith regime, and the desire of the new government to strangle any wealth the Europeans had by gradually refusing them to export any of their personal belongings, until eventually, if they wished to leave, they even left all their furniture and chattels in the country. I could see it happening, getting worse by each visit, but the Whites there were stuck there, hoping against hope that things would improve, and quoting that the 'Zim dollar would always be a dollar' – shades of Harold Wilson, British Prime Minister, quoting 'the pound in your pocket' as the IMF arrived. Their worst fears came true in a few short years, and by 1984 things were much grimmer for the Europeans.

On one such trip, I decided to take the train from Salisbury to Gaborone, via Francistown, in Botswana, for no other reason than my curiosity and to see how the trains worked. All was pretty basic, with carriages as one would see in a poor European country, and basic meals served at the bar. While having a beer there, I was incensed by the attitude of four Europeans towards the poor African server, whom they verbally abused to such a degree that I was about to attack them. I restrained from that out of cowardice, but was left in no doubts about the anger and frustration of the indigenous population with a certain faction of their 'superiors'. I flew from Gaborone to Johannesburg.

Meantime, back in Johannesburg, my new Afrikaner contact soon got to work, recruiting me to report back on such mundane things as the state of the crops, the general rumours, etc. during such visits. He seemed satisfied with my verbal reports, and coming on for Christmas, invited me to Pretoria for a special Christmas Day celebration. I drove to the address he gave me, which happened to be his headquarters at BOSS – Bureau of State Security. We had a few drinks there at a ridiculously cheap price before going to Loftus Versfeld Stadium, the Holy Grail of South African rugby, where a really sumptuous buffet was laid out – the best I ever saw. The afternoon was a pleasant surprise of eating and dancing with the many beautiful ladies among the several hundred invited.

Two weeks later it was payback time. My controller asked me if I knew Paris a little, and on answering affirmatively, he asked me if I would be interested in going there for about a week. No need to hesitate, so after a good briefing, I was on the plane, and on arriving in Paris, checked into a modest hotel, and began my work. I was to keep an eye on a gentleman from Port Elizabeth who had been invited by the French Government to discuss some points in his field of technical publications.

I checked out his hotel, saw him enter as he arrived from South Africa, and generally kept an eye on him through Thursday and Friday. On Saturday, he has free to sightsee, and like many tourists, headed for the Champs Elysees. At a coffee shop in a central gallery there, I contrived to sit at his table, as most of the others were occupied. He seemed happy to have an English speaker as company, and we soon got talking. I suggested a bus tour to best see the sights in a short time, and he willingly agreed. Later, he invited me to dinner and we choose a good restaurant. He explained that he was the guest of the French Government and that all expenses were for their account. That was fine by me. Here I was getting paid by the South Africans to keep an eye on him, while he was inviting me to dinner in a top restaurant at the expense of the French – a win-win situation for me!

Several days of such easy surveillance, going for a few beers in the evenings, while he told me of his days with the Government officials, passed without incident. There was nothing out of line as far as I knew, and reported well on the visit when I returned to Johannesburg.

By now, I was getting fidgety. It was a case of deciding once again as to where to set up – either South Africa or elsewhere! Political storm clouds were building up where I was, and not being happy with the apartheid situation there, I decided it was time to bid goodbye to Africa. I had many wonderful experiences, a few not so nice, but it was time to move on. I spent six weeks in the Irish Club in Eaton Square, London, while I sorted myself out, finally ending up in Houston, Texas, – but that's another story!.

Chapter 32

Strange stories! Welsh

Staying in the best hotel in Zaire, in Lubumbashi, the Karavia Hotel was a very welcome relief from the normal, and was quite a lot better than the Park Hotel in the town centre. The hotel was built by British Caledonian Airways, was modern and well run, with a nice pool to relax by, overlooking the nearby lake Kipopo, and bordering on the golf course.

Dinner was a semi-formal event in the restaurant, laid out with white starched tablecloths and napkins. One evening, I noticed a large round table laid out for about twelve persons, and was curious as to what group was coming. I did not have long to wait. A dozen young men came in, and surprisingly, all were speaking English, like real English people, almost! I quickly established that they were Welsh, which, as my curiosity got the better of me, and I turned around to ask them of their origin. They were more reluctant to give more specific details, vaguely saying they were from north Wales. On pressing them as to just where, they asked me if I has heard of Llangollen, to which I replied yes. Further questions elicited the information that it was near there, and on pursuing with my twenty questions, one finally said they were from Ruabon, a small village on the old A5 route to Holyhead. I asked them if they knew Jack a' Larry. The man on the opposite side of the table jumped up, saying "J.C. that's my cousin" Talk of small worlds!

Jack was the only local that I employed while putting a sewer scheme through the village, mostly in small 'headings' – small tunnels lined with timber boards, where pre-cast concrete pipes were placed, before being packed all around with concrete. He was an ex-miner, and a good worker. My acquaintance with Jack stood me in good stead. The gang were installing equipment in the copper mines nearby, and during my six weeks stay while they were there, I never had to pay for a meal or a drink. They simply signed for it, and it was charged to the Gecamines Company. I will never forget the immediate reaction of Jack's cousin – one of the really amusing encounters during ones travels.

More strange stories! Kisangani

While waiting for something to happen, to arrange for the next trip, or just wondering what or where to do or go, sometimes leaves one with a spare few days or weeks just kicking ones heels. It was one of those times that I wandered into the Mission base workshop, where the mechanic, a Brother of the order of the Mission, was working. He took care of the vehicles of the Mission, giving them the once–over when the priests arrived at the base from their outlying stations, which they did on a regular basis. He did all that was necessary, not just to the engines, but welding, patching-up and fixing whatever that needed to be done. During one of my visits, he was busy servicing the only Uni-Mog the Mission had in the north. We chatted a bit, and I spoke at length to the priest who drove it in – both he and the Brother/mechanic spoke reasonably good English. The priest told me of his mission; four days drive in the Uni-Mog, south of Kisangani along the Zaire River. He came into base once a month for supplies, but was the only white man for many kilometres. Apparently it was a very tough station. He usually stayed two or three days, and was off again when he had all the provisions that were needed. A Land Rover was not robust enough for the trip. After one such visit, I mentioned it after the communal dinner to the other priests present, and all agreed that it was a very tough station, and they obviously had tremendous respect for him. I was intrigued!

I happened to be at the base when he next came on his monthly trip. We had a great chat about the location of his mission, the hardships, and the life in general – light years from the 'sophistication' of Kisangani. When the Father had gone to chase up his stores, I quietly asked the Brother how well he knew the priest. He had heard the priest telling me some tales, and I was wondering if they were a flight of fancy. The Brother told me that he had known him for twelve years, and had never known him to tell a lie. I was in a fix! What to do? To go there would satisfy the adventurer in me, but to get there was another story. I neither had a Uni-Mog, nor the means to get one in the whole of Zaire, nor the money to buy one, had one been available. Most of the Uni-Mogs in Africa were imported from Europe, second hand, having been bought from local or regional government departments or the German army stores. That was out of the question for me, as time frame alone was several months to get it to Zaire. Unfortunately, I had to let the idea drop, much to my everlasting regret.

The Father had told me of tribes which came to his mission, maybe twice a year, from the deep jungle in the heart of the country. It took them about two weeks to get to the Mission, through a mix of jungle and swamp, to do their 'shopping' there. That was the precious commodity in many countries for thousands of years – salt! They traded their diamonds for salt, diamonds that were extra big, of very good quality. They had never traded with the Belgians, as they did not trust them. The Belgians had been very harsh colonialists, cutting off the hands of many of the Africans if they did not gather enough rubber, a practice that was mainly stopped after the report of Sir Roger Casement on brutality and slavery there.

The priest saw my interest, but was very discreet. He told me if anyone ever went in there, they might not come back, as it was whispered that the locals were still practising cannibalism. I think he wished I would take on the challenge. Asked as to when one could reliably expect the 'salters' to next come to his Mission, he replied that he did not know – one might have to wait four or five months. That was the final decider for me – I could not see myself waiting for several months at a Mission base in the jungle for Mick the cannibal to pay a visit.

About two months later, the big Bwana of the mission base approached me, and almost as an aside, said "it is true" and walked away. I puzzled over this for a day or two before approaching the Brother at the garage, and mentioned my inability to understand what the big Bwana was referring to. He simply said that he was referring to the priest with the Uni-Mog, and confirming that his stories, amazing as they sounded, were true.

It has been a dream of mine for many years to do that trip. Today, with satellite technology, one could beam transmissions directly from the villages in the jungle, where no white man has been. Coming out alive? I'd take my chances on that one!

More strange stories! Trailfinders

During my wanderings in Africa, first in Zambia, then in Tanzania, near Dar-es-Salaam, by Kunduchi beach, an ex-British army truck, a 4-wheel-drive kept crossing my path. They pulled into the camp site at Kunduchi a few days after my arrival. They were hot and dusty, fed-up with staring at each other over long hours and many kilometres on the back of a truck, with tempers about to boil over. They had come to the right place to relax and enjoy. The hotel/camp was a haven of tranquility, beautiful white beaches, clean, and stretching for kilometres. Fishing from a pirogue, a traditional log dug-out, was a pleasure, with many species of multi-coloured fish being caught by the hotel employees for export to exotic fish dealers in Europe. The fish were bagged in plastic, some water, given enough oxygen to last their journey, and flown out every weekend. The owner invited me to accompany them on their fishing trip, and he deposited me on an atoll while they continued their fishing. It was heavenly there, with soft white sand, plenty of shade under the trees, and not a sinner in sight. I swam, dozed and sunbathed until they collected me some hours later. Life continued like that for some days until I was getting restless again.

The Trailfinders and I were beginning to become friends by now, seeing the same faces over and over. We exchanged a few pleasantries, but I decided that with a large group present, it was time for me to move on.

I finally arrived in Nairobi, based in the Intercontinental Hotel, in a cabana by the pool. I was in clover! A (small) room by the pool at the hotel for half the price of a regular room was a prime spot for taking my pick from the many young ladies lolling around sunbathing. True to form, the Trailfinders truck pulled in some days later. One of the young ladies on the truck asked me if she could use my cabana to clean up, and afterwards, we shared a beer. She told me she was living in London, but of Scottish ancestry. Her father was a laird in Mull, off the west coast of Scotland.

Ownie was a neighbour of mine in Ireland who trained boxers in the local hall, doing a good job of it, with two Irish champions coming from his school in my time. In later years, he was dry-ditching (an ancient method of building stone walls without any cement or other filling). He made good money at this while working in Mull, off the west coast of Scotland, and had his half page photo in an Irish Sunday newspaper, showing him working and earning eight hundred pounds stg. per week – a small fortune in those days.

I asked her, tongue in cheek, if she knew Ownie. She did. He worked for her father building stone walls! That sealed a nice friendship. Ownie was delighted to hear, on my return to my home village, that people had heard of him as far afield as Kenya.

Finally! The Aaiwee Bird

Many years ago there was a terrific drought in Kenya, where much of the wildlife died, and virtually the only trees that remained standing were the Baobab trees – the massive big trees that absorb huge amounts of water, do not grow very high, but have enormous fibrous trunks. Many of the animals – those that survived, were mere skeletons, pure skin and bones. It was during this period that many of the birds headed south in search of water. Among them were strange birds which went to the savannah lands of Katanga, and settled there. The abundance of food and water there was the deciding factor for them; they liked it so much that it became their new home.

The food was so plentiful that they did not have to scavenge for it, as it was all around them, with no shortage of water, and they wanted for nothing. Little by little, they lost the power of flight, due to their lack of use of their wings. This did not create any great problem for them, except when they wanted to have a small change of scenery during the winter season there. They then had to find their directions to get to their destination, but their wings could no longer support them in flight. They only had enough power to rise above the elephant grass to see where they were to go, rising up just high enough to see their way, before flopping to earth again owing to their lack of use. It was at this point that the local Africans called them the Aaiwee birds, as they did not understand the bird language, birds which had come from an English speaking area many years previously in Kenya, when the birds arose over the elephant grass, looking around, shouting 'where are we?' 'where are we?'

Printed in Great Britain
by Amazon.co.uk, Ltd.,
Marston Gate.